MW01114128

FINDING KATE

By Jean Morris Long

COLD RIVER STUDIO
NASHVILLE, TENNESSEE

Cold River Studio is an independent press committed to introducing fresh, exciting voices to the reading public. It is our mission to take a chance on deserving authors and achieve the highest quality when bringing their words to the marketplace. We believe in the power of words and ideas and strive to introduce readers to new, creative writers.

Published by Cold River Studio, Nashville, Tennessee

www.coldriverstudio.com

First Edition: August 2011

Printed in the United States of America
ISBN 978-0-9828146-9-7

To my husband, Bill, who journeyed the miles with me through Virginia and Arkansas tracing Kate's steps, copied whole books for my research, proofed endless pages, guided me through the frightening electronic maze of my computer and most of all encouraged me when the mountain seemed too tall.

CONTENTS

INTRODUCTION

There comes a time, as we grow older, when we become curious about our family history. Genealogy is the number one hobby in America. People spend hours in libraries, courthouses, and now on the Internet, searching through census, birth, death, and marriage records to find their ancestors.

I was not particularly interested in the past when I was young. My eyes glazed over when my Aunt Annie Latané Morris (Beard), who seemed to be a thousand years old at the time, pulled out her dusty books and papers bearing the records of our family history. Her vast knowledge and deep family devotion were evident, but only when there was any mention of her mother and my paternal grandmother would my ears perk up with curiosity.

I knew that her name was in the great, thick genealogy book *Lewis of Warner Hall, A History of the Family and Their Descent From Other Early Virginia Families* compiled by Merrow Edgerton Sorley, the recognized authority on the Lewis family:

> "Catherine Lewis, married a Mr. Morris and resided in Keo, Arkansas. They had several children."

In the distinguished volume of Lewis family members, my grandmother warranted little more than two lines. She was listed by Sorley as the ninth child of twelve, born in 1863 to Thomas Waring Lewis and Ann Ursula Latané in Tappahannock, Virginia. Their ancestry is traced back to Councilor John Lewis and Elizabeth Warner of Warner Hall, the established ancestral home of the Lewis family.

My father was one of my grandmother's four living children. She died in 1907 when she was forty-four years old and my father was ten. When my mother spoke of her, she straightened her shoulders and lifted her chin with pride, "Your father's mother was a Lewis from Virginia. She came to Arkansas to teach school as a young girl." The tone of her voice changed to one of reverence as my mother spoke the words "Virginia" and "Lewis." In her mind, Virginia was a sacred place, steeped in tradition and culture. She felt that descendants of the Lewis family bordered on being royalty. Our lives on a small, dusty farm in Arkansas were greatly enriched by this knowledge.

I had always sensed that there was something brave and romantic about my grandmother, even though I knew little of the actual events of her life. For as long as I can remember, I had heard about the other distinguished members of her family: George Washington's sister had married Fielding Lewis, the brother of my grandmother's ancestor, Charles Lewis. The great grandfather of Meriwether Lewis—of the Lewis and Clark Expedition—was also my grandmother's great, great, great grandfather.

"Waring is a name that has been in every generation of our family," I remember hearing my mother's voice proclaim. Waring was my brother's middle name, as well as his son's.

Much later, at the University of Virginia Library, I would discover that William de Warrenne arrived in England from France with William the Conqueror. De Warrenne married William's sister and became the first Earl of Surrey. His name was later Anglicized to Waring. My grandmother's maternal great grandfather, William Latané, married Ann Waring, a decendant of this line. It became evident that the Lewis and Latané families were intertwined throughout their histories.

William Latané was the grandson of Parson Lewis Latané, a French Huguenot priest who fled to England from France following the revocation of the Edict of Nantes and who matriculated at Queen's College, Oxford, in 1691. Upon the completion of his training, Parson Latané was ordained by the Bishop of London and commissioned to preach in the colonies. In 1701 he sailed to America and headed up the Rappahannock River to become the priest at South Farnham Parish, which later evolved into St. Paul's Church in Essex County, my grandmother's family church.

During the American Civil War, a member of the Latané family was memorialized for his bravery in a painting titled *The Burial of Latané*. An exquisitely aged steel engraving of the original hung in our living room. Its large and elaborate gold leaf frame took a place of honor over our best brocade couch. Guests who questioned the somberness of its subject were told the tragic story of the death and burial of my grandmother's uncle, Captain William Latané:

> On Friday June 13, 1862, the brave young physician led his squadron as it smashed against the

Union Army on a road near Old Church in Hanover County, Virginia. He was the sole fatality that Stuart's 1,200-man band suffered that day. He was the first of three sons my grandmother's grandparents would lose in the Civil War. Captain Latané's brother carried his body through enemy lines to reach Westwood Plantation where the women and slaves buried him.

When poet John R. Thompson heard this story, he was inspired to write a eulogy to Captain Latané's gallantry. The poem in turn inspired noted artist of the day, William D. Washington, to paint what became a symbol of the Southern cause. Hundreds of steel engravings of his rendering were found in homes throughout the South. It featured a group of elegantly hoop-skirted women and one lone male slave gathered around the grave of this fallen Confederate soldier; he was denied the company of male mourners who were busy fighting battles close by.

Among our other revered ancestors were ministers, lawyers, doctors, soldiers, and leaders in the government of our young country. My grandmother is among all of the family listings, but there are never any details of her life. She just seemed to have disappeared in Arkansas. I knew her well-established lineage but nothing about *her* except that she came to Arkansas to teach school. Her story remained a mystery until my father brought home the letters.

Finding Kate

LETTERS TO LUMIE

One day a stranger appeared at my father's office with fifteen letters from my grandmother dated from 1885 to 1888 and addressed to her friend Lumie Hudgens in Pine Bluff, Arkansas. The yellowed pages were handwritten on both sides with faded sepia ink and tied together with a pale blue satin ribbon. They were all signed "Kate." My father never had an opportunity to meet the person who brought the treasure to his office. Perhaps it was a relative who was going through Lumie's possessions and found them. Lumie's father had been a prominent member of one of the communities where Kate taught school. Goodspeed's *Biographical and Historical Memoirs* stated that, "Miss Lumie Hudgens was the daughter of John A. Hudgens, of Jefferson County, whose name is too well known to need any comment." John Hudgens had six children and, by necessity, was interested and involved in obtaining teachers for their education. As was the custom at the time, my grandmother must have lived with the Hudgens family when she first came to teach school in Jefferson County. She and Lumie became very close friends and faithful correspondents. Some of the letters were post marked from Raineyville and Plum Bayou, Arkansas, two of the three school locations where Kate taught from 1885–1890. Others were rich in the details of her family life, written from her home in Virginia where she stayed between teaching positions in Arkansas.

I remember when my father gave me the letters; I was honored by his trust and felt a great sense of responsibility for preserving them. I was in college at the time and almost the same age my grandmother had been when she wrote them. I kept them in my bedside table drawer. When I was home for holidays or summer vacation, I read the letters late into the night. From the beginning, I felt that Kate was writing to me:

> *I am sitting all alone in front of a blazing fire & my thoughts have wandered instinctively to all of you. As I cannot walk in and have a pleasant chat, I will resort to pen.*
>
> (Raineyville, Arkansas, February 9, 1885)

Right there in my bedroom, when all of the rest of the world was asleep, we got to know each other. In the letters, she told me about everything from what she was wearing to her latest hairdo. I found one picture hidden deep in a worn velvet album of long-forgotten relatives. From that photo she stared at me with bright, hopeful eyes. Her innocent young face was rimmed in curls while the rest of her hair was pulled back and up, into a soft roll crowning her head.

> *Here in Virginia the hair is right on top of the head. You rarely ever see anyone with their hair low. I fix mine up and you can't imagine how becoming it is. I wish I had fixed it so before I left Ark. I look about*

two inches taller.
(Mansfield, Miller's Tavern, Virginia, January 1886)

She made me laugh when she described the frustrating attempt of one of her Virginia beaus to call upon her. His name happened to be Haile.

I have had Haile Storms right often lately. He started here last Saturday evening but was caught in a storm and drenched to the skin, only got as far as Miller's and waited till the storm was over and went back home. Mr. Haile ought not to mind a storm, ought he?...I ought to be ashamed for I don't care whether he comes or stays, Lumie, he is the first beau I ever had and "Madam Rumor" says he has returned to his first love.
(Mansfield, Miller's Tavern, Virginia, June 29, 1885)

Kate told me about the glorious Christmas holiday with her Virginia family and dancing until two o'clock in the morning. She described the wedding of her best friend in exquisite detail. She seemed delighted and quite proud to be playing the organ on Sundays at her beloved St. Paul's Church. She must have been a talented seamstress, for she showed no modesty in her account of how beautifully she made her latest outfit, copying the pattern from a picture in a newspaper.

In contrast, when Kate was in Arkansas, her letters were about simple gatherings such as a small group of neighbors assembling to sit with a sick friend to be sure he received his medication at regular intervals during the night. Her description of the joy she found in this ordinary event was written with the enthusiasm of a child, as natural as though she were talking to me. I found her caring, optimistic, trusting to a fault, rather daring for her time, inventive, strong willed, and extremely independent.

Kate maintained a sense of humor. I liked her intensely. I was touched by the sincerity of her words. Underneath the seemingly lighthearted frivolity of her youth was a deep, unshakeable faith in God and wisdom beyond her years. I will long remember reading a passage in one of her letters to Lumie just at the right time in my life to inspire and guide me. Once, in college, when I thought my heart was irrevocably broken by an older suitor unworthy of the depths of my young devotion, I found these reassuring words from Kate:

> *...just try to say and feel that our kind heavenly fa-ther knows just what we need, and He never sends a single pang in anger...I tell you this for I have tried it and felt what a loving Father I have...I have sought for boons in an agony of tears and felt that life would not be worth living without them, but when the years had passed and I could look back on events, I have had cause to thank God that he denied me.*

(Mansfield, Miller's Tavern, Virginia, September 15, 1885)

I knew that Kate would understand perfectly and deal with my youthful and perhaps trite dilemmas with great compassion.

> *Your trouble and unhappiness to some might appear trivial, but my child I know just how to sympathize with you. You will know how much I felt when I tell you that when I finished your letter, I "went off" and indulged in a good cry.*

(Mansfield, Miller's Tavern, September 15, 1885)

When I was planning my own wedding, I imagined that we would have talked over the choice of my wedding dress. I was sure she would have rejoiced with me in my happiness.

> *I suppose you are busy as a bee now getting ready for your wedding. "Lum's Wedding!" How funny it sounds. I wish I could see your outfit. I know it will be lovely and I think your wedding dress will be bewitching.*

I presumed she would have reminded me of the important things when my life seemed too busy.

> *Lum, do you ever think of Him who sends you this happiness? Do you not thank Him? We have had many talks about your being a Christian. Don't you remember what you told me one evening when we were out walking, that when you were married you would give your heart to God. Remember now, you have not yourself alone to act for. You are compelled to exert an influence over him.*
> (Mansfield, Miller's Tavern, Virginia, May 13, 1887)

Kate would have encouraged me to look for the good and make the best of a situation.

> *I don't believe you are as cynical on the subject as you make it appear, are you? I suppose most people at times have a feeling of utter loneliness, as if there was no one who quite understood or appreciated them, then all we can do is to turn resolutely and look for the sunshine; it is surely shining somewhere.*
> (Stafford, Mississippi, November 23, 1889)

Kate's letters remained in my bedside table long after I moved away from home. Somehow they found a safe place in my new home when I married and had a family. They were tucked in the corner on the top shelf of my closet for another thirty-five years, but Kate was always there. I gave her name to my only daughter, Mary Katherine, who passed it on to her daughter, Katherine Latané. My son named his first child Rebecca Katherine.

Kate's correspondence with Lumie began when she was only twenty-two years old and continued until 1890 just before she met my grandfather. My grandmother remained twenty-two years old to me, frozen in the time capsule of her letters while I was busy with my own life, husband, and young family.

As my family grew up, married, and moved away, I was suddenly aware of my own mortality. I felt a great urgency to find out more about this lady who had become so much a part of my life. It was then that I decided it was time to go back to Kate's home state of Virginia to search for answers.

RETURN TO VIRGINIA

One of Kate's younger brothers, born in 1867, the next to last of her eleven siblings, was Reverend Thomas Deane Lewis, professor of Biblical history and literature at Sweet Briar College and chaplain of the college for many years. He was one of the reasons that I attended school there even though he had died many years before I arrived. While I was at Sweet Briar, I came to know his son and namesake, Thomas D. Lewis Jr., who by then was living in Richmond. He was truly a blessing to me. Though he never knew my grandmother, he knew more about the Lewises and Latanés than any other member of the family he so dearly loved. He lived to be over ninety years old and had a brilliant mind and bright eyes that always sparkled with pride when he spoke of the family history. We had corresponded through the years, so when he arranged for me to be invited to attend the Warner Lewis family reunion in 1985 in Virginia, my husband and I made plans to be there. It was the ninetieth anniversary of another Lewis reunion held in 1895 at the Lewis family home, Mansfield, which had celebrated the eightieth birthday of Kate's father. During this 1985 family gathering, I recognized the great sense of family pride that existed among all of my newfound relatives. They, however, maintained a quiet assurance of their stature that had little to do with monetary wealth but all to do with the value of their faith, education, and obligation to their fellow man. That day, Thomas read a most appropriate quote from one of his father's letters:

> *A noble linage is not something of which to be proud but for which to be thankful; it is not something to fill us with complacency but with a desire to be worthy of our heritage.*

(Reverend Thomas Dean Lewis to
Thomas Dean Lewis Jr., July 9, 1936)

It was on this trip to Virginia in 1985 that I began to delve into genealogy with new energy. I traced the Latané family back to the Huguenot Parson Latané, and the Lewis family to Charles Lewis, Captain in the Virginia Regiment's 1755 campaign against the French and Indians, commanded by his cousin, the Honorable George Washington. Through my efforts, I gained membership in The National Society of Colonial Dames of America and Daughters of the American Revolution. It was with great satisfaction that I was able to obtain proof of the stories that I had heard all of my life about noted family members in American history.

On future return trips to Virginia, my husband and I drove to Charlottesville and had the privilege of entering the library at the University of Virginia, where boxes of letters and artifacts under the Lewis and Latané family names are kept. Proud family members had managed to save these priceless treasures. There I found family letters in French that spoke of shipments of tobacco, prices, and lists of slaves. Parson Latané had attended Oxford University in the seventeenth century, and I was able to see his sheep skin diploma. It was an extraordinary experience for my hands to touch this symbol of his distinguished education. It was almost impossible for me to imagine that a beautiful manuscript, which traced the Waring family's ancestry, inscribed in perfect block lettering, could have been done by human hands. Perusing some of these documents, too numerous to comprehend, I acquired a tremendous insight and familiarity with the family—far beyond anything I had gained from an empty lists of names.

In 2004, when I attended my fiftieth college reunion at Sweet Briar College, I visited Warner Hall, the original estate of the Lewis family in the Tidewater region of Virginia. Portions of the home had burned, but it had been rebuilt and expanded over the years. It was in a sadly neglected condition before a couple from New York decided to retire in Virginia and manage a bed and breakfast there. After extensive renovation, they were able to recreate the grand and gracious setting of long ago. When my husband and I visited Warner Hall, we found the graves of many of our ancestors in the vast yard leading down to the Severn River.

The promotional material for the hotel described the scene:

> Ideally situated at the head of the Severn River in Gloucester County, the manor house at Warner Hall stands on a neck of land that has been occupied and built upon continually from the mid-seventeenth century. Referred to as "Austin's Desire" in the 1642 land patent, the original six-hundred-acre plantation site was established

by Augustine Warner as a "land grant" from the British Crown. Augustine Warner received the acreage in exchange for bringing twelve settlers across the Atlantic Ocean to the Jamestown settlement, a colony desperately in need of manpower to survive in the New World.

Augustine Warner Sr. died in 1674, and his only son, Augustine Warner Jr., inherited the estate but died at an early age. Warner's daughter, Elizabeth, married "Councillor" John Lewis. They continued as lord and lady of Warner Hall until her death in 1719. The two families associated with the property from this early period until well into the nineteenth century were the Warners and the Lewises, among the most prominent families in Colonial Virginia. Warner Hall Plantation thrived, as did the descendants of Augustine Warner. Some of the most recognized names in American history are direct descendents of Augustine Warner— George Washington, the first president of the United States; Robert E. Lee, the most famous Civil War general; and Captain Meriwether Lewis, renowned American explorer of Lewis and Clark Expedition. Washington was a frequent visitor to his grandparents' plantation. Queen Elizabeth II is a direct descent of Augustine Warner through the Bowes-Lyon family and the Earl of Strathmore. In England, Warner Hall is referred to as "the Home of the Queen's American ancestors." In 1957, shortly after her coronation, Queen Elizabeth visited Warner Hall in conjunction with her trip to Jamestown for the 350th anniversary of its settlement.

Warner Hall is also significant for the part it played in the drama of Bacon's Rebellion, one of the most important events in early Virginia history. After leading a 1676 rebellion against the British governor and burning Jamestown, Bacon retreated to Warner Hall Plantation. At the time, Augustine Warner II, who was speaker of the House of Burgesses and member of the king's council, was in residence and very likely agitated that his plantation was taken over by opponents of the Crown.

Today, Warner Hall consists of a Colonial Revival manor house (circa 1900), which was re-built on the earlier seventeenth and eighteenth century foundation. Like the previous structure at Warner Hall, all of which indicated the prominence of their owners, the Colonial Revival core is a grand architectural gesture. The original seventeenth century west wing dependency (the plantation schoolroom and tutor's quarters) has been completely restored and offers a rare glimpse into the past. Historic outbuildings include eighteenth century brick stables, a dairy barn, and smokehouse. The Warner-Lewis family graveyard, maintained by the Association for the Preservation of Virginia Antiquities, offers a remarkable collection of seventeenth and eighteenth century tombstones.

Today's Warner Hall is a lovely old home with a massive staircase leading to the upper floors. We stayed in the only first-floor bedroom, appropriately named The Washington Suite. It was a regal room with a fireplace, writing desk, and comfortable chairs. Before retiring, I pored over the historical information readily available to guests. I then slept peacefully in the plush king-size bed surrounded by the familiar family ghosts of the past.

These were all rich and rewarding discoveries for me and, in a sense, had much to do with Kate's family pride and confident independence, but this was not where I would find Kate. I had been distracted by the distinguished and celebrated members in her family history. I knew that I must get back to Kate's own story in Miller's Tavern, Virginia, where her life began.

PILGRIMAGE TO KATE'S HOME
IN ESSEX COUNTY

By 2004, Kate's letters were a hundred and nineteen years old. That year, I wrote to my cousin Thomas and explained that I would like to come visit Kate's birthplace—where I thought I might have an opportunity to speak with some of her immediate remaining family, children of her eleven brothers and sisters.

Upon our arrival, Thomas and his wife, Molly, gathered together some of Kate's grand nieces and nephews who were still alive and living in the Richmond area. During our lunch, I was able to observe how much many of them resembled Kate's faded picture. Unfortunately, none of them seemed to know anything about Kate. They were of another generation. Since Kate had left Virginia in 1885 for Arkansas to teach school and hadn't returned except for temporary visits back home, the relatives who might have known her were gone, and all traces of their accounts of her life were buried with them. I watched each one of these relations, carefully searching for a mannerism or a tiny clue to gain an insight into what Kate was like or how she talked and laughed. I thought I caught a glimpse of her here and there among the cousins, most of them endowed with Kate's red hair: a legendary Lewis trait.

As the small clan told the stories of their own childhoods, I recognized some familiar phrases that I found in Kate's letters, such as "I reckon" and "I declare." I sensed the same charm and humor that I had found in her written words. Even though I was disappointed not to gain personal stories about Kate, I realized that meeting them was an important part of knowing her. They were very interested in my quest and took great pains in helping to identify some of the names Kate mentioned in her letters. Their kindnesses endeared them all to me, especially Thomas.

In the dining room of Thomas' home, I found the familiar steel engraving of the *Burial of Latané* hanging in its place of honor in the dining room. I had no doubts that all members of the family also had a copy in their homes. Engravings of William D. Washington's painting were in Southern homes from Missouri to Maryland. After Kate married and settled into her home in Arkansas, she wrote to her sister in Virginia,

> *I am so glad to get my copy of the Burial of Latané. I*
> *want to take it down next week and have it framed.*
> (Little Rock, Arkansas, February 9, 1898)

Only when I had read these words did I realize that this was our family copy and that the beautiful frame I had long admired was the one Kate had selected in Little Rock, Arkansas, over a hundred years before.

The next day, Thomas drove us from his home in Richmond, Virginia, to Miller's Tavern, where Kate grew up. It is a small community, located a few miles from Tappahannock on the Rappahannock River, sixty miles from Richmond on today's modern roads. Unfortunately, Mansfield,

Kate's childhood home, had burned long ago, but we drove by the landsite, an empty vacant field, on a beautiful spring morning. I tried to visualize what it would have been like as I remembered one of Kate's letters to Lumie when she was in Virginia for the summer. It expressed all of the joy of being home again. The heading was written in bold script with a big exclamation point: "HOME!"

> *I think my home is just as sweet as it could be. Our flowers are lovely and the corn right in front of the house is beautiful...I wish you could see our home. Just wait until next summer!*

(Mansfield, Miller's Tavern, Virginia, June 29, 1885)

In 1957, The Women's Club of Essex County published a charming little book called *Essex County Virginia: Its Historic Homes, Landmarks and Traditions*. It described Kate's home, Mansfield, where her seven brothers and four sisters had been raised and where she lived until she moved to Arkansas:

> *Mansfield* was the home of Thomas Waring Lewis and his wife, Ann Ursula Latané. It was situated about two miles south of Miller's Tavern. It was an estate of 400 acres formerly owned by the Manns. The house was built in 1856. It was a two-story frame building of sixteen rooms and a basement. The house burned in 1893. The location is marked by a small building in the yard which was built of the timbers from "Mann's Ordinary," one of the old taverns of the pre-Revolutionary period which stood upon the premises. Gordon

15

Lewis, a grandson of the builder, is the present owner. (p. 47)

The same book also describes, *The Meadow*, built in 1823, which was the home of Kate's maternal grandparents, Henry Waring Latané Sr. and Susanna Allen:

> The house was a handsome two-story building of eleven rooms, including the basement. Under the roof was an eighteen-inch cornice and there were dormer windows in the attic. The house rested on a four-foot brick foundation. It had a high medium-sized porch in front and at the back. There were large double doors opening into the hall. A closed winding stairway led from the back of the hall to the second floor... All of the original beaded poplar weatherboarding was said to have come from one tree. Hand-wrought nails were used. The tall chimneys at each end of the house were unusually handsome. They were eight feet at the base, their dimensions decreasing to six feet at the second story and to four feet at the top. (p. 39)

Kate's home, that of her grandparents, and many of those featured in the booklet on Essex County Homes could well have been the setting for the parties such as the ones Kate mentioned when she wrote to Lumie of her glorious Christmas holiday in Essex County, Virginia:

> *I have never spent such a Xmas in my life, if it will not tire you; I will give you a description and shall expect you to do the same when you write to me.*

*Well, to begin: Christmas day we had about
14 to dine with us. That night we were invited to
a party 6 miles from here. We all went in the car-
riage. You know we don't mind distances here, to my
great delight, when I got there I found there would
be dancing. I just had a lively time. There were some
very nice fellows who danced well, so of course, I
enjoyed it. Sis Nannie and Lucy would not dance
at all during Xmas. We got back home about three
o'clock. Monday night I was invited to another, but
that was 9 miles and I thought it rather too far to
ride in the night, then the rest of the week we had
pound parties around at the different houses in the
neighborhood. Everyone who went carried a pound
of something so you see it did not cost any one much.
I went every night, Tuesday, Wednesday, Thursday
and Friday, every night I danced till about 1 o'clock.
Oh my dear, I did have such a delightful time but every night I would wish for you. Each night before the
dancing began, I had engagements up to about the
14th set and we never danced over twelve.*
(Mansfield, Miller's Tavern, Jan. 5, 1886)

Although Kate was only seven when her mother died,
she was nurtured with great abiding love by her four older
sisters and seven brothers. Mr. Lewis never remarried and
the family remained faithfully close and supportive. Ann
Suzanna Lewis was called Nannie by Kate and her other
sisters. She was eldest daughter and fifteen years older
than Kate. She wrote to Kate in Arkansas:

What you said (in your letter) about our home life

> *at dear old Mansfield was very true, the loving in-*
> *fluence and sweet associations are held dear by each*
> *one of us.*

(Miller's Tavern, Virginia, June 29, 1885)

Much later, when Kate's father died, she wrote to Nannie from Arkansas:

> *I could picture him so plainly sitting in the old arm*
> *chair. I can see the rooms and furnishings of the old*
> *house...My heart clings so to old associations and*
> *have spent so many happy peaceful hours in the old*
> *chamber. When I read the Psalms you don't know*
> *how many of them bring up a bright sun shining*
> *room and I seem to hear Pa's voice reading...That*
> *influence and those memories have kept me up all*
> *those years I lived on the farm and had no outside*
> *help to make me good...*

(1400 Arch Street, Little Rock, Arkansas,
February 1898)

Kate missed the spiritual inspiration and the support of her Virginia family and church.

In the years that followed General Lee's surrender ending the Civil War, the Essex County economy tried to recover from a war and the economic disaster it had brought. Though Kate's father farmed several hundred acres, James Slaughter wrote in his *History of Essex County* that the rich planter was extinct and nearly everyone was a poor farmer. Patrick Waring lamented in 1875: "the farmers are having up hill work...little capital, poor land and small prices are hard to contend against...Corn, long the leading crop in Essex, dropped from 466,000 bushels in 1860 to 250,000 in 1870. Growing cotton, wool, tobacco, honey, butter, and other cash crops had turned into subsistence farming" (p. 212).

Federal troops had plundered the supply of horses and stock. The farming depression would keep Essex County severely pressed for generations.

Slaughter's book also emphasized the importance that the people of Essex County placed on their religion: "Next to survival and government, the worship of God was the most important priority of the Rappahannock River pioneers" (p. 18).

In all of her letters, it is evident that St. Paul's Episcopal Church was a great part of Kate's life and those of her ancestors. On my visit to Virginia, Thomas drove us the short distance to Kate's beloved St. Paul's Church, which remains a very active and vital church. The Essex County Women's Club book describes the historic old church:

> Erected in 1838–39, the church is located 10 miles west of Tappahannock on Rt. 360. It boasts of Gothic style embellishments on their traditional rectangular forms. Parts of the ruins of the Old Piscataway Church were used in the construction of St. Paul's. The vestry was added in 1924, and it retains the rural simplicity of clear glass Gothic windows and its Hobart unconventional pulpit. Its tall windows with their hand-carved casings, jambs and sashes are outstanding for their Gothic beauty. Double paneled blinds secured by four-inch bars protect the windows. The communion table is handmade

to harmonize with the pulpit, which is paneled black walnut. It is still an active church today. (p. 42)

At the time of my first visit, a history of St. Paul's was in the process of being written, and the young female rector let me spend the afternoon with all of the records that were to be used in that undertaking. I found Kate's confirmation date and a record of her marriage there. Among Kate's things, she had saved a letter from Arthur Temple, written at that time of her confirmation at age thirteen. Temple had, for many years, served on South Farnham's Parish and St. Paul's Vestries. His niece had married Kate's oldest brother, so he was considered a part of her family. Kate's mother had died when she was seven years old so he felt it was his responsibility to counsel with her:

My dear young friend,

Since witnessing the tranquility and peace with which your now sainted mother went to her rest, have you not with one of old, said, "Let me die the death of the Righteous & let my last end be like my mother's"? I love to be with a Christian who has strong unwavering faith when about to leave this world and pass into eternity.

It encourages us to hope that when we shall come to die, we may also hope to dwell with God in that rest which he has promised to all those who love Him; & become the faithful followers of Christ.

I trust from the sentiments you expressed to me when I spoke to you with reference to becoming a Christian some time ago, you have fully determined to enter at once fully the work of being a faithful soldier of the cross early in life-such determination, made in humble reliance upon God to assist you in carrying out this delightful undertaking, will give you true peace of mind.

I hope you are already earnestly engaged in a contest for a crown of Life: I think by God's gracious assistance you will be entirely successful!

We are told in scripture "Angels are ministering spirits"—think of your mother's being commissioned to come on such an errand to minister to you while engaged in earnest prayer to God for spiritual guidance in your progress Heavenwards!

I have some valuable works for young Christians if you would like to read some of them, I will look them up and hand them to you.

I hope you read your Bible regularly: asking the influences of God's Holy Spirit to enable you to be entirely decided in choosing the Lord.

Remember, Dear....positive determination to consecrate yourself to the work of preparing for an inheritance among the saints in glory!

You are just at an age to enable you to make a wise choice and make you the child of God and Heir of Heaven. Oh, do not fail to give your young heart and warm affections to God who is now offering you a crown of Life!

I shall daily pray that you may make a wise choice: who saved with an everlasting salvation!

God says, "They who seek early shall find me,"

Sincerely & affectionately
You friend & relative in hope of Heaven,
Arthur Temple

Written at the top of the letter was a postscript, undoubtedly added later:

> *I rejoice to learn from our beloved Pastor that you profess to be a child of God. May your path Heavenward be brighter and brighter till the perfect day!*

In contrast to her uncle's earnest but gloomy Victorian prospective, Kate had a deep sense of joy in her life on this earth and her devotion to church. During my visit to St Paul's, I walked where Kate had walked up the aisle in that beautiful old church with the white painted pews and balcony stalls once designated for the slaves. The quiet sanctuary was empty, but I felt Kate's presence there. I could almost hear the music as I remembered her letter to Lumie when she was home for the summer.

> *I play the organ at St. Paul's now. Last Sunday, I heard Mr. Meade complimented me very much and you know how proud I felt...When I got home, I found they did not have any music at all in the Sunday School, did not have any books, so I wrote on directly ordering a lot, did not wait to have the money collected, advanced it myself. I got the "New Life." They had never seen the collection before and are very much pleased with it. I know most of them in the book now. I have practiced a good deal since I've been home.*
>
> (Mansfield, Miller's Tavern, Virginia, 1885)

Thomas and Molly took us outside to the cemetery, which seemed to surround and protect the church building. There we found the graves of Kate's mother, father, grandmother, grandfather, brothers, and sisters, almost all there but Kate. There in that place, I was touched by the impact of the loneliness she must have sometimes felt in Arkansas, so far from all of her family in Virginia.

Our next destination was the Essex County Court House, which was described in Slaughter's *History of Essex County*: "...built in 1848 to replace the old original, largely of a Greek revival design with some Federal qualities. A 1926 renovation, largely financed by Alfred DuPont, added a bell and clock tower. The courthouse has long contained the largest portrait collection in the county with portraits of scores of Essex leaders from the past two centuries adorning its walls" (p. 105).

On the walls of the old courthouse, in the portrait gallery, I found faces to go with the family names I had encountered in my search. There was a stone plaque memorializing the deaths of Kate's three uncles, distinguished heroes of the Civil War. I found a portrait of Kate's maternal grandfather, Henry Waring Latané, Gentleman Justice Legislator. A copy of this painting had always hung in my parents' home and now hung in my own. Until that day, none of us had known the identity of the distinguished gentleman who stared from his prominent position in our dining room all of those years through eyes that strangely resembled my father's.

The records in the courthouse, dating from 1655, were hidden in private homes during the Civil War. I was therefore able to find Kate's birth certificate, her marriage license, and her father's will. I discovered for the first time that Kate's official name was Catherine Lewis, spelled with a "C." For me, however, she would always be Kate, as she signed her letters.

I was unable to find any record of where Kate attended school. James B. Slaughter, in his *History of Essex County*, wrote that until the early 1800s, education for all American girls centered on Bible study and ornamental arts such as music, dance and embroidery. Girls were deemed incapable of the higher levels of instruction that boys received after age fourteen. Slaughter went on to applaud Essex County's forward thinking attitudes toward the education of women. He explained their existing progressive attitudes toward women's education. One of its citizens, James Mercer Garnett, began writing and lecturing on the role of women in his 1824 publication *Seven Lectures of Female Education*. The work established Garnett as one of the foremost advocates of improving education opportunities for women. His wife, Mary Mercer Garnett, opened Elmwood, one of the first schools in Virginia that taught young women the full range of academic subjects at the time. Her advertisement outlined the curriculum:

> Reading, English Grammar, Writing, Arithmetic, Geography, and the use of the Globes. Also Belles Lettres, the elements of Chemistry, of Natural and Moral Philosphy, the Latin, French and Italian Languages, with General History.

Another girls' school, The Tappahannock Female Seminary, became a highly respected academy there until 1860, three years before Kate was born. The success of these two schools later prompted the opening of several other Essex county schools for women (p. 128–129).

Whatever the financial situation during the ravages of the Civil War, Mr. Lewis found the means to educate his seven boys. He had attended Rappahannock Academy, one of the oldest private schools in the river valley. Kate complained of finding it difficult to concentrate on writing her letter to Lumie while her younger brothers were "reciting their Latin." These brothers would later attend William and Mary College, Washington and Lee University, and the University of Virginia; three of her brothers became physicians, two Episcopal ministers, and one a lawyer. It seems that Mr. Lewis was also diligent in the education of his five daughters.

Reverend and Mrs. McGuire operated an all-girls boarding school in Tappahannock during the time Mr. Lewis' daughters were growing up. A copy of an October 1866 bill from this school, which Kate's older sister Lucy attended, was among the Lewis letters that I had acquired from the University of Virginia Library archives. The statement not only gave the prices but promised that:

> *Ample provision is made for the comfort of the pupils and for their thorough instruction in the several branches of a complete English education; in French, Latin and vocal and instrumental Music. Competent and experienced assistance has been engaged.*
>
> ### *Terms Per Half Session*
>
> *Board and Tuition in English....................887.50*
> *Tuition in English..............................17.50*
> *Tuition in Latin................................7.50*
> *Tuition in French...............................7.50*
> *Tuition in Music (Instrumental)................15.50*

Vocal Music, at Teacher's charges
Primary Department: Tuition 12.50

Another letter from Kate's oldest sister, written in 1873 from Mansfield when Kate was ten years old, says,

Papa carried Susan to Tappahannock yesterday to go to school to Mrs. McGuire, it was a great struggle with her to leave home but she will no doubt be well satisfied after getting acquainted with the girls. Lucy is teaching the children here this session and she has become so fond of it that I reckon I will give up the school entirely to her.

As recorded in the Essex County Historical Society's newsletter, "Tiny" Haile attended Hansbrough's private school in Orange, about sixty miles from Tappahannock. "Tiny" was about the same age and a close friend of Kate. From these clues, I surmise that Kate was schooled by her sister Lucy during her younger years at home and received an above average education in one of the available girls' schools in the area.

Wherever she received her education, when Kate left Virginia around age twenty-one, she was qualified to teach school in Arkansas. Possibly due to the economic conditions after the Civil War, girls no longer had the luxury of staying home and doing the embroidery. Kate mentions the number of young girls in her community teaching in various surrounding states and consequently finding husbands there, much to Kate's concern in one of her letters to Lumie,

We all went up to St. Paul's today and spent the day in decorating the church for Tiny Haile's marriage which

will take place to-morrow morning. She will marry a man from Ga. He came to-day. I got a glimpse of him as he passed the church. The couple will go directly off on the boat. I have wandered off from the decorations in the church, right in front of the pulpit there is a large arch covered with evergreens and then almost covered with bright geraniums and roses, then right in the middle of the arch, suspended just over where the couple will stand is a large bell, that was lovely beyond description, it was a perfect bell shape, covered with ivy leaves, not a colored flower about it, the tongue was three pure white lilies with a few green leaves. I tell you it was perfectly lovely. The arch looks like a rainbow. I say it is the bow of promise.

...Tiny did not have any couples to wait on her, but just before she entered church, I with one of her cousins walked in, keeping time to a march on the organ, had to walk the entire length of the church. I believe I was almost as much excited as she was. Everything passed off beautifully. The, bride looked lovely in her traveling suit. Directly after the ceremony was over the bridal couple left for their home in Ga. Next Wednesday night I will wait on Minnie Temple. I never heard anything like the marrying that is going on now. Nearly all the girls who went off last session have had beaus on to see them. I counted up to nine, some of them from S.C. and Ga. Several have asked me if I will not have a friend from Ark. to visit me, say they know I will not let him come. Well, such is life!

(Mansfield, September 1885)

Poor Kate! There was no "him" to come for her from Arkansas and she was feeling left out. By the time she wrote the letter, she had already been teaching in Arkansas but had not come home with a potential husband. She, however, would not feel sorry for herself long. She would use her time between teaching positions in Arkansas to become the organist for St. Paul's and join the reading club.

> *We had a meeting of the Reading Club here two weeks ago. I wore my blue dress for the first time since getting home. I mean my party dress. I was appointed to read that night and you have no idea how I dreaded it. I read a selection from The Golden Gem on Friends. My voice trembled a little for two or three lines, but they said I got on alright. We enjoyed being at a sociable that often.*

She helped with her new twin nieces when her sister Mary returned home from out west. She baked a chess cake and sewed clothes for herself and her sister.

> *I have been sewing a great deal lately. I have made three dresses, one of them a nice worsted dress, a Mother Hubbard night gown and a nice underskirt besides helping about other sewing. Sis Sue had a dress made for traveling at the same time I was making my nice dress when she got hers home she was dreadfully dissatisfied, said it was not made near as nicely as mine, really the dress was a complete botch. I saw how much put out she was so I took it and fixed it over for her and it looks all right now. The woman tried to make it by a picture in a magazine, the same I made mine by, but she made a failure in*

*the drapery of the overskirt. I am afraid you think
that sounds right conceited but everybody says my
dress is made so much nicer than hers.*
(Mansfield, 1885)

Kate was willing to make the best of it, but cooking
and sewing were not satisfying her. She was determined
to return to her job in Arkansas. It was time for her to
make her own way.

TEACHING IN ARKANSAS

I t was the fall of 1885 before Kate was given another teaching position in Arkansas. In one of her later letters she describes her trip from Virginia to Arkansas, which took five days. She took a boat up the Rappahannock River from Tappahannock to Fredericksburg then to Washington and down to Little Rock by train. The whole country had an amazing system of railroads at the time. As early as 1887 Arkansas boasted over 2,000 miles of railway. Kate could have traveled by train all the way to her next teaching position in Raineyville, Jefferson County, Arkansas.

The school system she was re-entering was disorganized and inadequate. Goodspeed's biographical history of Jefferson County gives a detailed view of the slow and misguided educational development there:

> Before the Civil War, Arkansas had no law providing a direct property tax to finance the schools. Jefferson County pioneers had seldom found time and facilities for more than the meager educational advantages for their children at home. Aside from parochial school, it is not certain there were any schools of note before 1841. Though the deplorable conditions as a

free common school system, the people of the State were by no means without educational facilities. From the very beginning, the more or less thickly settled communities had what was known as "subscription schools" taught by "itinerant" or traveling schoolmasters, usually for a period of three months for a stipulated price per pupil...

By an act approved May 18, 1867, the legislature made a marked forward movement in the cause of education...The act stipulated that a tax of 20 cents on every $100 worth of taxable property should be levied for the purpose of establishing and maintaining a system of public schools. The second section made this fund sacred to be used for no other purpose whatever. The fourth section provided for a superintendent of public instruction and defined his duties. The eighth section provided for a school commissioner to be chosen by the electors of each county who should examine any one applying for a position as school teacher: granting to those qualified to teach a certificate without which no one could be legally employed to teach...The congressional township was made the unit of the school district, the act also setting forth that in the event of the trustees failing to have a school taught in the district at least three months in the year, the same thereby forfeited its portion of the school revenue. When these wise and liberal arrangements were made, it must be remembered by people bankrupt by war and suffering the hard trials of reconstruction...

The fact that many school officers can neither read nor write has left the reports of the county in lamentable condition until very recently, when some improvement has been manifest. One preserved account made in Jefferson County in 1885, [the year Kate would have been teaching] reported ninety-six teachers of whom sixty were male and thirty-four female. In 1888 there were ninety-five teachers of whom seventy-three were male and only four female. In 1885 the monthly wages ranged from $35 to $60. In 1888 none were above $47.50. There were thirty-one school houses, one brick and thirty wooden ones in 1885. (p. 138–141)

The first letter that I have from Kate, written to Lumie in Pine Bluff, Arkansas, was postmarked from Raineyville, Arkansas. Raineyville, or Rainey, which was located a short distance from Pine Buff.

Kate's comments about her school are mostly concerned with extending her current school term or finding a position for the following year. Her employment was most likely with a subscription school as described above, with the term lasting only until the funds were exhausted. Though she seems to have been employed by families of means who either boarded her at their homes or found accommodations in comfortable surroundings, she had little job security or financial stability there. Oftentimes her salary was paid in warrants or vouchers.

I could not get my contract fixed up in time to begin school before the first Monday in January. I have ten scholars on the role now. There are two Negro directors of the school and last Two of them, Isaac Dowd, paid my school a visit. I had to be very polite to him and wish you could have seen the airs he put on. I was afraid my schoolhouse would be blown away. He examined the first Reader class. I suppose he could go no higher.

(Raineyville, Arkansas, January 18, 1885)

Another letter from Kate written that spring is one of the few times she complained of her teaching responsibilities.

I only weigh 110 pounds, everybody says I look badly. I don't wonder at it for these bad children are enough to kill a body. What you all said about my going home had more truth in it than I knew. I thought I was engaged here for the 10 months but Mrs. Rainey told me this evening that they thought the Public school would last 6 months and that Mr. Rainey could not afford to employ me after the Public school is out so there I am left. I think I shall try to get the Cerlin's school house so I can stay here till summer. Mrs. Rainey told me she would help me all she could. Ask Mrs. Hudgens to send me some message about my warrants, whether they bear any better value since the taxes are being collected.

(Raineyville, Arkansas, March 2, 1885)

Kate had problems with her teaching salary, but she enjoyed the social activities in Arkansas. They may not have had as elaborate parties, but she was just as satisfied with what she called candy "stews." The mixture was made from dark molasses, brown sugar, vinegar, butter, and soda boiled until it began to harden. It was then poured onto buttered platters until it cooled enough to handle a small quantity at a time. The young people spent hours pulling and tugging at the mixture, giggling with delight. The longer the candy was pulled the whiter is got. When the gooey mass hardened, it was placed on the counter, ready to break and eat.

> *Mr. and Mrs. Morrow have given me two candy stews at Mr. Hinson's. They did not have any one but Wilsie and me. I had lots of fun pulling the candy.*

(Raineyville, January 18, 1885)

> *I have some good news to tell you too. I will not be like the Irishman and save the best for last but will begin at it. Well, what do you reckon it is? Mrs. Hinson is going to give me a party next Friday night. We are counting on you all, Dikydemus is going to carry invitations down that way and you have just got to come. I am looking forward to it with so much pleasure. The hours seem like days till Friday comes...I have promised to help Mrs. Hinson set the table and so on that evening. You all come straight here and we can all primp together.*

(Raineyville, February 9, 1885)

The same letter describes her sitting up all night with a sick friend. A whole group came over and joined her. Where a group was gathered around Kate, it became a party.

Last Friday night Mrs. Hinson stayed all night here.
Wright was sick and we had to give him medicine every
two hours so she came to sit up with me after supper.
Dr. Morrow, John Bene and Dikydemus came. They
stayed till eleven. I tell you we had a lively time.
When Dr. and John Bene left, Dick stayed and sat
up with Mrs. Hinson and me. Wright was not sick
enough for us to sit in the room with him. We only
went into give him medicine. We all three sat up here
till four o'clock and I declare there was scarcely a
pause in the conversation. We talked party from the
word go and we told ghost stories enough to scare a
half dozen men. About twelve, Mrs. Hinson and I
went in the kitchen and got some coffee, light bread
and butter. We toasted the light bread, each one was
his own cook. You ought to have seen the fun.

Kate was unable to work out a contract for the next
year. This newspaper clipping was sent to me from her
granddaughter in Texas:

Miss Kate Lewis, who has been teaching school
in Raineyville, this county, left yesterday for her
home in Essex County, Virginia. Miss Lewis is
an accomplished and popular instructor and
made many friends while here.

Kate had returned to Mansfield in Virginia on June
2, 1885, when she wrote to Lumie about how much she
missed all of her Arkansas friends.

I never close my eyes that I do not dream of some of
my Arkansas friends. I hope I can get schools there

as long as I teach for I like the Arkansas people better than any I ever was with and hope I have some true friends among you. Do you ever hear the Raineyville folks talk about me? I hope I will not be "out of mind" as soon as out of sight...Mrs. Hinsen wrote me there was to be a party at Mr. Marshall's last Friday night. Did you go? A right remarkable coincidence happened that evening just after dark. I was sitting on the porch alone and it seemed to me I could just hear "Old Mose" playing "Little Ladies" and all the tunes he plays kept singing in my ears, his waltz tunes. I told some of them that night, "I'll bet they are having a party in Ark. I feel just like it."
(Mansfield, Miller's Tavern, June 2, 1885)

In a September letter of the same year, she urged her friend to help her find another position in Arkansas.

As the fall comes on I feel as if I ought to go to Arkansas...I have one champion at least in Mrs. Hudgens. Tell her she must talk up for me on all occasions. I will certainly have to come back there next fall. Pa and sister Nannie don't want me to teach at all, but if I can get a place in Ark. near you all, I will certainly come, if not I will not teach at all. So you all must look out for a school for me if you want to see me. I hope Miss Scotty Oliver will not teach at Mr. Tucker's next fall and I can get that place.

Kate did eventually find another teaching post in Arkansas. In April of 1888, she wrote Lumie from Plum Bayou, Arkansas, only a few miles from Raineyville. She was within a twenty- or thirty-mile radius of her old friend, but she was not quite so pleased with the town itself. The area was not nearly as genteel as her past positions.

> *The saloon is in sight from here and I tell you every*
> *Saturday it is a perfect Babel over there, fighting,*
> *shooting off pistols etc.*
> (Plum Bayou, Arkansas, April 4, 1888)

In contrast to this report, a March 19, 1888, newspaper clipping saved by a cousin in Texas told a different story about Kate's activities in Plum Bayou, Arkansas. (Note the flowery prose of the time.)

> At Cozy Nook, the residence of Mr. and Mrs.
> J.A Miller, a delightful evening was passed on
> Thursday, the 15th.
>
> The entertainment was complimentary
> to Mr. George Purves, of Scotland, a nephew
> of Mrs. Miller. Young and old of the pleasant
> neighborhood attended and an evening of rare
> enjoyment crowned the efforts of the charming
> hostess with unrivalled success. The devotees
> of terpsichore wondered through the mazes of
> joyous dance until about eleven o'clock with
> a delightful repast was served, after which we
> were favored with charming vocal music from
> Miss Lewis and Mrs. Dunlap, both masters of
> the art and a recitation from Miss Nichol added
> to the enjoyment of the evening...
>
> The "iron tongue of midnight" had tolled
> the holy hour and hushed into silence ere the
> guest departed. The ride home of course was

joyous lighted on our way with the silver lamps
of heaven hung by angel hands. The regrets of
many follow Mr. Purves on his homeward journey for while in our midst he won many warm
friends whose best wishes attend him. May an
early return to the shores of America be mysti-
cally veiled by the future.

I have often thought it strange that I never found any
of Lumie's letters to Kate. I often wondered why Kate had
not saved them. Perhaps they were somehow lost. There
is one last letter from Kate that might explain the absence
of Lumie's side of the correspondence. Although I can
never fully know the circumstances, undoubtedly Lumie
accused Kate of spreading a rumor about her. Questioning
Kate's integrity provoked the anger of the feisty young lady
with red hair and exploded in her indignant reply to Lumie.

You who have known me nearly five years & know
that I have lived as everyone true woman will live,
far above any such thoughts. I do thank my God
that He, not man will be my Judge. I have no idea
what the "ridiculous tales" you refer to nor do I care
to know. My own conscious innocence is sufficient
and I know all who really loved me will not for an
instant believe them. There comes a time in the lives
of most of us when there is a broad dividing line
between the fair weather friends and those who are
true at all times. Farewell. Kate Lewis
(Mansfield, Miller's Tavern, August 17, 1888)

Kate might have destroyed all of her friend's letters the

very day she ended their friendship and correspondence with the one final letter to Lumie.

Before leaving that part of Kate's life in communities near Pine Bluff, Arkansas, I felt that I should explore this part of the state. I grew up only twenty miles from the area where Kate first taught and had known Lumie, but I had not been there since my early childhood. Until I read her letters, I had no idea the schools were located in that vicinity. It was time to see where she first lived in Arkansas. One early spring day, when my husband and I were visiting relatives nearby, we decided to take the road toward Pine Bluff and locate some of the places that she mentioned in her letters.

It was in the early spring before planting began. The land was flat, stretching as far as we could see across treeless and desolate farmland. As we came near Plum Bayou, we looked across the field and saw a large abandoned two-story house with majestic columns. Its wooden siding was gray with age and the sagging roof seemed on the brink of caving in. I had to wonder if the once impressive structure might have been one of the homes where Kate attended the "Candy pulls" or danced to the fiddle of "Old Mose" during its former grandeur. There was nothing else in sight and no one to ask in the few decaying stores along the highway.

Seven miles down two-lane Highway 51 is Tucker, Arkansas, which was once called Raineyville, named for the Rainey family. Kate mentioned the Tucker family in many of her letters. Today, Tucker has the dubious distinction of being the site of the Arkansas State Penitentiary. There was no searching for old familiar locations there, so we passed by the high security fences and drove on toward Pine Bluff.

During Kate's time near there, Pine Bluff was a thriving river town with a port where cotton-filled boats docked on the Arkansas River. Originally the Quapaw tribe lived on this high riverbank, forested with pine trees. Later, Europeans settled on this safe haven from flooding where they founded the town of Pine Bluff in 1832, two years before Arkansas became a state.

According to historian James Leslie, Pine Bluff entered its "Golden Era" in the 1880s with cotton production and river commerce helping the city draw industries and public institutions to the area, making it, by 1890, the state's third largest city. The first telephone system was placed in service March 31, 1883. Wiley Jones, a freedman who achieved wealth by his own business, built the first mule-drawn streetcar in October 1886. When Kate lived in the surrounding communities in 1890, the population was 9,952.

She kept in contact with many of her friends from this cultured and rather sophisticated little community long after she married. My husband and I stopped by the library to research names in her letters before a drive through the quaint old portion of the town, which had survived the years quite well.

On the way back toward Little Rock, we left the highway and drove down a dirt road in the middle of a cotton patch. Under the shade of a pecan tree, we talked with Wardel and Ruby Dowd, a black couple who had lived there in their modest house some seventy years. They spoke of the Tucker family and where the remaining members might be living. They took pride in the fact that their ancestor was an administrator in the school system and perhaps the very one that Kate mentioned during those difficult Reconstruction days. Of course, we could find no witnesses who had known my grandmother, but on that day in the warm spring sunshine, I felt her presence.

COURTSHIP AND MARRIAGE

I had come to the end of Kate's letters to Lumie. I had returned to Kate's family home and traced her childhood in Essex County, Virginia. Kate had remained ageless in those letters to Lumie, a lighthearted young girl. Now it was time to go back to Arkansas to find Kate as a wife and mother. She had grown older, and I had grown older with her.

I knew that she had four children in Arkansas who were all deceased, so I wrote to my cousins, as well as their children and grandchildren, asking for more letters or clues that they might have concerning Kate. Each of the children of my father's three siblings was able to provide a valuable piece of Kate's puzzle for me.

Kate's only daughter, Annie, had always been the family record keeper. She had one living daughter in Houston, Texas, who graciously shared several epistles addressed to Kate in Arkansas from her brothers and sisters in Virginia. She had one letter in Kate's handwriting to her sister in Virginia after she married. The two Arkansas newspaper clippings quoted previously were among the treasures she shared with me.

Edward's oldest daughter contributed invaluable pictures, letters and family history. When we sold my parents' home, I saved a stack of random letters among my father's things. As I dutifully shuffled through the words of unfamiliar acquaintances, I discovered some correspondence between Kate and my grandfather, written during their courtship while she was teaching school in Stratford, Mississippi. My father had never shown me these letters. I smiled at the formality as I read my grandfather address his letter to "Ms. Kate," and she addressed her correspondence to "Mr. Morris." After their marriage, she wrote, "My darling husband," but her references to others regarding him were always formal.

By now, I had spent hours transcribing Kate's letters to Lumie. With a magnifying glass and great patience, I typed out each word. I felt it was my responsibility to save them. My research continued in Little Rock at the Arkansas History Commission Library where I browsed through the history of education in Arkansas. By accident, I discovered an old ledger journal on microfilm that belonged to my grandfather. The tedious records, faithfully inscribed in pencil, consisted of one brief line per day. Half of that was a daily weather report, but its conscientious reliability traced in detail the major events in Kate's seventeen years as his wife. My cousin Lewis Dean Morris, who owns a farm and an antique store in Keo, had my grandfather's original crumbling diary stored inside his office safe. He cautiously entrusted it to me.

On May 13, 1888, my grandfather, William Nathan Morris of Keo, Arkansas, made his usual brief one-line entry in his ledger diary. This was his first mention of Kate:

> *S13 Clear & cool from W with Miss Lewis &*
> *back to W*

The "W" stood for Waring. Kate's paternal grandmother was a Waring, so Kate's father's middle name was Waring. There are several accounts of Lewis relatives in Arkansas. Many enterprising Virginian kin (before Kate) had followed land grants and left the parental fireside to explore new territories. Kate's sister Sue once lamented in a letter to Kate,

I do trust that James does not take off for Arkansas.
We have so many of our loved ones there already.
(Miller's Tavern, January 5, 1901)

This Waring was probably one of those relations who had introduced Kate to Mr. Morris. The Sunday after the first mention of Kate, Mr. Morris called on Kate again at Plum Bayou, which was about ten miles from his home in Keo.
S27 Cloudy went to see Miss Lewis. Spent a
pleasant day.

Twenty days later, he squeezed two written lines into the customary single space of his ledger.
S16 Very hot went with Miss K. Lewis to Dr.
Donelson's Made love to Miss K. was rejected
big rain and storm
M18 Much depressed in spirit on account of above
Hot showering from Dr. Donelson's home
F22 Miss Kate Leaves for home leaving me much
discouraged Very hot rain in eve from Dr.
Donelson's to neighbors

Again, I can never know what occurred between the couple nor why Kate "rejected" him at that point in their relationship, unless he was proceeding too quickly.

These few brief notes in his diary in May of 1888 are the first clues to a connection between my grandfather and grandmother.

The bereft suitor was described in Goodspeed's *Biographical and Historical Memoirs, 1889*:

> Now just in the prime of an active and well spent life, is a successful agriculturist of this region. He was born in Stewart County, Tennessee, in 1850 to the union of Rev. James T. Morris and Eliza (Weeks) Morris. Nathan Morris passed his boyhood days at home, until he became of age, shortly after which he bought an improved farm and commenced life for himself. Active and preserving in his adopted call, he now owns 1,300 acres of land in this county, in different tracts, about 400 acres of which are under cultivation: 445 acres of improved land comprise the home farm and where he resides, enjoying wide respect. 1886 he built a cotton gin and now has one of the finest gins in this part of the State, fitted throughout with new machinery. The following year he built a saw-mill, and at this time is engaged also in getting out lumber. Mr. Morris is a member of the Masonic order and belongs to the Methodist Episcopal Church. He is public spirited and energetic and a life of honorable deportment has gained universal esteem. (632)

This information led me to Stewart County, Tennessee, where county records reveal that William Nathan Morris was the second of seven children born to James T. Morris and Eliza (Weeks) Morris. His birth date was 1845, rather than 1850 as falsely given in the Goodspeed biography.

Sometime between 1850 and 1852, William moved with his parents and family from Stewart County, Tennessee, to Arkansas.

Arkansas State Archives microfilm, petaining to Clear Lake, card number 45029, list both William and his father as members of Clear Lake Independent Guards of Prairie County, Arkansas, for local defense, under Act of Congress, October 13, 1862. The descriptive list dated June 1, 1863, reords a brief sketch of them both:

James T. Morris
Age: 54
Color of Hair: Sandy
Color of Eyes: Gray
Height: 6ft.

William Nathan Morris
Age: 17
Color of Hair: Red
Color of Eyes: Brown
Height: 5ft.7in.

At this young age, my grandfather went on to serve in a Confederate Unit during the Civil War. His youngest brother, Edward Everett Morris, a well-know Presbyterian minister in Arkansas, wrote down many of the family stories told to him by his father. His written words, titled, *Genealogical and Historical Sketch of the Name and Family of Morris*, were later typed and passed out to the Morris clan. Included in these seven-and-a-half unpublished pages was an account of his brother, "Nath's," return to the devastation of his father's home and farm after the Civil War. The land was all that was left. All of the mules and horses were gone. Only cattle and hogs remained on the range. This brief description reveals a great deal about the spirit and determination of my grandfather and Kate's future husband.

> ...Brother Nath knew the situation at home. He was in the Calvary down in Texas when the news came that Lee had surrendered to Grant and that the army would disband that night...It was free for all grab. Get what you can of what is left...As brother Nath passed through Louisiana he came upon a plantation home where a party of some kind was in progress. He noticed that in the barn lot there were many mules and he remarked to his companion, 'Those are Confederate mules and I have as much right to them as they do.' He went to the lot and picked out several mules and rode away. Several men were on the porch watching but they made no move to stop him.
>
> ...Before he got home he got another horse, making six mules and a horse...His other brother, Jim, got home on the horse he was riding. They had six head of mules to cultivate 150 acres of farmland...and came to Little Rock and borrowed from a bank $2,000.00 and gave a mortgage on the six mules and the crop.

Even though it was the month of May and very late to plant a crop, my grandfather and his brothers were successful that year and their wealth increased as they gained more land. William Nathan's lessons came hard. He had to be tough and inventive to survive. Acquiring land was an important part of building a reputation and gaining a position of prominence in this young, untamed land. The land became the focus of his life.

In the two-volume version of *The Letters of an American Farmer* by J. Hector St. John de Crevecoeur, published in 1882, this French immigrant turned American farmer expressed his own fervent enthusiasm for the unlimited advantages of land ownership:

> I never return home without feeling pleasing emotion…The instant I enter on our land, the bright idea of property of exclusive right, of independence exalt my mind. Precious soil, I say to myself…no wonder that we should thus cherish its possession, no wonder so many Europeans, who have never been able to say that such portion of land was theirs, cross the Atlantic to realize that happiness.
>
> The formerly rude soil has been converted by my father into a pleasant farm and in return, it has established all our rights: on it is founded our rank, our freedom, our powers as citizens, our importance as inhabitants of such a district. These images, I must confess, I always behold with pleasure and extend them as far
> as my imagination can reach. (96–104)

William Nathan's passion for the land and farming consumed his days. That obsession was passed down to the next generation. His three boys remained on the land their entire lives, and his daughter's husband ran the mercantile store in town, which thrived on farming incomes.

Though a small part of Edward's memoires cover the story of his brother's return from the Civil War, most of his word-of-mouth history is about the adventures of their father, James T. Morris. Edward portrays him almost as a legendary figure of amazing physical stamina, determination, and deep religious convictions. He surely had a great influence on the character of his son William Nathan.

Edward relates,

> Born in 1809, James T. Morris was a member of the Cumberland Presbyterian Church and early became a candidate for the gospel ministry. He attended Princeton College at Princeton, Kentucky, and became a home missionary, holding great camp meetings over a great part of Tennessee where hundreds and thousands were converted. It was not an uncommon thing to preach 2 and 3 hours at a time and come out of the pulpit with clothes wringing wet with perspiration, the spirit of God fell upon the people, saint and sinners. Some sinners fell prostrate in the aisles and all over the great congregation. Many crowded the altar, many fell before they could reach the altar. Results: 300 souls were converted to God. It was like the day of Pentecost when 3000 souls were saved.
>
> Dr. A.R. Winfield, editor of the Arkansas Methodist, of Little Rock, said to me, "Your father was one of the greatest preachers of the

great preachers of his age. He had great talents:
he was wonderfully and powerfully gifted."

James T. Morris must have been quite a charismatic
and colorful character. He had ventured forth to California
in search of gold in 1849 before he came to Arkansas. My
great Uncle Edward continued his memoirs:

> The trip to California was a great and notorious
> event his life. I have heard him talk about it for
> hours at a time. He never tired telling about it. It
> seems that he and his party went by way of the
> Isthmus of Panama. I am quite sure they came
> back that way through Central America. Those
> from the north and east went by ship down the
> Atlantic Ocean and around Cape Horn in South
> America and up the Pacific to San Francisco,
> where all the gold seekers landed. From there
> they went up the Crooked Joaquin River to Tule-
> berg, now Stockton, California, and then on foot
> north 30 miles to the gold fields. I do not know
> how long Father and his two slaves were in the
> gold fields nor what success they had in finding
> gold, but I judge they were measurable success-
> ful. Anyway, evidently Father felt that the two
> young Negroes had earned their freedom from
> slavery for he manumitted both of them. One
> accepted his freedom with gratitude. The other,
> Harry, would not take his freedom but decided
> to stay with Father and returned home.
>
> On the return home...an epidemic broke
> out among the passengers and almost every

day one died. Burial service, which consisted in sewing the body up in a bag of some sort or without a bag, placing the body on a plank and heaving it overboard in the ocean. This was accompanied by prayer and talk by Father. One day the Captain of the ship said, "Parson, for God's sake do not be serious in your talks. You will run us all crazy!" Father replied that it was a time to be serious when nearly every day they were launching a soul into eternity.

…passengers carried their gold in large belts buckled around their bodies. One night father awoke and saw a man slipping along and following the sleepers to see if he might find a belt loose he could get. Father watched him until he got nearer and raising up he said, "Stop you thief, if you come nearer and I get hold of you, I'll cut your throat!" The thief disappeared quickly…

Family legend assumes that he did return with enough gold to purchase the land that his sons extended to a new generation. He lived near his children until his death in Lonoke County, Arkansas in 1887.[1]

After the Civil War, James T. Morris' son, William Nathan Morris, settled on the land and began his life as

---

[1] It is interesting that some of the details of Edward's memoirs on his father have been researched by a devoted family genealogist, Pat Dakins. She discovered that there actually was a Princeton Seminary in Kentucky at a time when James T. Morris could have attended. Also she found his name on the passenger list for the vessel Oregon returning from Panama in 1850. The time frame fits the legend about his presence at the Gold Rush.

a farmer. His days were filled with cotton, droughts, rain, and travels by horse, buggy, or train from his farm to Little Rock, the county seat in Lonoke, Tucker, Pine Bluff, or even Memphis. His parents, cousins, and brothers lived nearby, but as a young man, there was no mention of a wife. An 1880 census shows an Inez Scott living with her family in Eagle Township, Pulaski County, Arkansas. She married my grandfather in 1881 when he was thirty-six and she nineteen. A brief line in his diary, which I discovered much later, confirmed the fact that she died in 1882, probably in childbirth.

S 13 My dear wife departed, 10:45

Mr. Morris remained single until he found Kate. The courtship lasted two years and most of that was through correspondence.

After the unhappy encounter between Kate and Mr. Morris in May of 1888, she went home and stayed in Virginia for a year. Among my father's things, I found a letter to Kate in Miller's Tavern, Virginia, from Mr. Morris during this interim. There must have been a letter of apology from him to which Kate had reluctantly and briefly responded.

> *It is apparent from your perforation that there are others as well as myself who are deficient in time and I judge from the brevity of your letter that you are one among them. I wish I could supply you but the "article" (time) being very scarce in this sector, I am unable to do so. You seemed to be in an excellent humor when you wrote. I therefore cannot account for the shortness of your communication. I was very much elated to know that I had been partially for-*

*given and hope ere this reaches you, that you in your
kindness of heart have entirely erased from memory
the fact of my ever having to sue for pardon. I shall
do all I can in the future to restore myself in your
confidence for you are the only one who has ever
awakened my heart to an appreciation of woman's
worth. I would say more but the confidence you reposed
in my having been so fearfully shaken, admonishes me
to desist until I am assured of your entire forgiveness.*
(Keo, Arkansas, October 16, 1889)

The next letter is postmarked Stafford, Bolivar County,
Mississippi, November 23, 1889, and is from Kate to Mr.
Morris. She had by now come back from Virginia to a town
in Mississippi very near the Arkansas state line. She was
disappointed by the scenery there, but she accepted the
inconveniences with a happy heart, knowing it might
mean riding a horse.

*Since getting acquainted I like it here much better.
There are some very pleasant people in this neighborhood, but the mud is so terrible we can't do much
visiting...I may get some nice horseback rides when
the buggies cannot go. I had rather ride horseback
than eat Xmas turkey. I thought the Ark. mud was a
bad as it could be, but it was not a circumstance to
this. You asked about my school. I expect to teach till
June, if I do not have chills before that time.*
(Stafford, Mississippi, November 23, 1889)

Kate was by now twenty-six years old and Mr. Morris
was forty-four according to the date of his birth found in

Stewart County, Tennessee records. In the family copy of Goodspeed's Arkansas biographies, the printed date has been overwritten in ink to read, "1845" which would make Mr. Morris eighteen years older than Kate. Many of these biographies were self-written, so perhaps Mr. Morris had stretched the truth a bit from the true census figures. I wondered what Kate thought about the age difference. She once wrote to Lumie about Lumie's engagement to an older man.

> *I am always very candid and you asked me to say what I thought of your "Man of Men." You know I always told you I thought it silly for a man of his age to address a child, but everyone is entitled to his opinion.*

(Mansfield, February 21, 1887)

Kate wrote to Mr. Morris of a "disinterested friendship" and tried to convince him that such a platonic relationship between a man and woman was possible. She seemed to have understood Mr. Morris' character from the beginning and did not hesitate to be "very candid" again!

> *I have amused myself very much at your want of time. You would like to hunt up a companion, but have not the time. Now what inference would a girl draw from this, only this: that if you succeeded in "finding" one, your life would be too busy to bestow on her the little attentions a woman cannot live without. Have you thought of that? I heard in the fall you did (not) have time to draw a long breath, and I became uneasy for fear you would die of asphyxia.*

(Stafford, Mississippi, November 23, 1889)

Perhaps Kate should have followed her first instincts about Mr. Morris. His business obligations would never allow him to give her the love, laughter, and affection she had known at Mansfield, but their correspondence continued. Kate's common sense and practicality was wavering a bit under Mr. Morris' persistence.

> *I have thought of you very often since getting your letter; whether I shall ask you to come or not. This hesitancy is because I fear I may wrong you, may give you needless pain. After what has passed between us, I might as well be perfectly frank with you and would be, if I talked to you, but it is hard to write just what I want to say.*

(Stafford, Mississippi, October 16, 1889)

There is a short message in January from Mr. Morris. He was coming to call on Kate in February of 1890. Undoubtedly his visit was quite successful for he writes,

> *You are all the world to me. I love you much more now than I did before I came over to see you. I had somewhat forgotten you. It brought you back to my mind as you were where I last met you when I had so little hope of ever gaining your affection. I now feel that I have at last gained them and your confidence. Although you have told me little of your love, yet I have the utmost confidence in you. I now feel that the dark cloud that has been looming above me for the last two years has at last disappeared and my skies are now cloudless. I hope that time will soon come when I call thee mine. There is not one in this wide*

world that I would rather call by that sweet name
wife than your own little sweet self.

(Keo, Arkansas February 28, 1890)

Since I don't have Kate's letter and thoughts during
this exchange, I must presume from his letter that Kate
was confused and unsure of this relationship at that time.
She remained reticent about announcing their betrothal
to the world. The next month Mr. Morris wrote,

> *You stated you have people blind as to our engage-*
> *ment. You have played it pretty well if you can keep*
> *from telling it to all of your friends for I can hardly*
> *keep from telling myself. I feel sometimes like telling*
> *every one that I love my Kate and am proud of it.*

(Keo, Arkansas, March 23, 1890)

Kate's sister had asked that Mr. Morris accompany
Kate to Virginia on her next trip home. Obviously, the family wanted to meet him. Kate also grew up on a farm, but
her father was what has often been called a "gentleman
farmer" with more than adequate labor for his small op-
eration. I must wonder if she understood when Mr. Morris
declined the Lewis invitation. Farming has always been a
total commitment. A good farmer has to seize the moment
that nature provides. There are no optional delays for a
successful crop, and Mr. Morris was very successful.

> *Tell her I am afraid I will have to disappoint them*
> *for I don't think I will be able to spare the time. June*
> *will be a time when I will be very busy with the crops*
> *and saw mill...what did your Pa say about your*
> *going to be married? I expect he is a little afraid to*
> *trust you with an Ark. Man. I guess he is not afraid*

*to risk your Judgment in the matter and will not
give himself any uneasiness about it. When shall I
ask him for you, don't you think I ought to? I hardly
know how to ask him. What shall I say to him? I
have a good mind to write him this Eve while I am
all alone.*

(Keo, Arkansas, March 23, 1890)

In the same letter, he mentioned the engagement ring.
She would have to forgo the pleasure and excitement of
a personal presentation. Even his apology on paper has to
be cut short because he has to get back out to his morning
farming routine.

*I fear that you may feel a little doubtful of me some-
times on account of my seeming negligence, please
don't entertain such a doubt for there is nothing on
earth that could make me forsake or prove else to
you...I will send your ring soon but would rather
have given it to you direct but if it will add to your
happiness I will send it soon...Kate, have to close as
I am stealing the time this morning when I ought to
be out now.*

The month of May was even busier for Mr. Morris. On
May 23, 1890, he wrote,

*I had my Photo taken when I was up town [Little
Rock] and will send it as soon as I get it. They will
not be ready for me until Monday. I got you a pretty
ring and will send it also. Have you an express office near you? If so give me directions how to send.
I am a little afraid to send by Exp office...When I*

come over to see you I shall only be able to spend a day or so with you. That will be a very busy season with me and it will be impossible for me to stay long. I will not be able to get there before the middle of July on account of having to attend court at Lonoke (the county seat of Lonoke County)...You stated that you like a country home. I am proud to know you do but I am afraid you will not like this one of mine. I know that you will be disappointed when you see it. You will find no society at all and I know you will soon want to go to town then. If you are like the other ladies that have been accustomed to society. I hope you will be satisfied and contented for a few years until we get in a little better shape financially and then we can go where you can have society. I hope you will be like I am and not care much about society.

"Run, Kate, run!" I want to say as I read these letters that she had so carefully saved among her treasures. Kate had grown up surrounded by a large, loving family who had always provided a gracious social life among old friends. Mr. Morris' words, however, were persuasive.

It's for you that I am living. I think of you nearly all the time. I expect much more than you do of me for I can think of you when I am riding about thro the field. Your name checks me often when I get fretted and keeps me from doing and saying things to be good so I can tell you what a good influence you have had over me...I imagine I would be so happy with you and have you to go riding with me every day in the field. I feel that you are a great little some-

*body. Can't help it. I saw a pretty young lady when
at Lonoke. Some think I (am) smitten with her. I do
think lots of her but when I come to compare her to my
sweet little Kate and her grand and noble qualities, she
comes very short of my standard woman...I think
there is none other living like yourself and feel more
certain of that every day of my life.*

(May 28, 1890)

On June 6, Mr. Morris cut his toe and chose to let it heal
on its own due to his busy farming life. An infection set in and
he had to have his toe amputated in Little Rock. He stayed
in the Grand Central Hotel, Mrs. S.C. Emmerson, Proprietor,
at 5th and Louisiana. He wrote to Kate that he was suffering
greatly and was confined to his bed for ten days,

*...longer than I ever kept bed in my life so you may
know it goes very hard with me. I am whittling while
lying on the bed...don't be uneasy...Remember and
pray for me... I did not get much attention from the
proprietors of the hotel...I imagined that if you had
been there I would have gotten well much sooner so
If I am ever to be afflicted again, it will not be until
we can be together and then I know I would be cared
for better than anyone else could do it...Your next to
last letter made me shed tears when you made such
an honest confession that you love me better than you
had ever loved anyone. This is the first time you have
ever made such an open confession. It seems to me
that you have been afraid to do so. I felt that you
ought to have done so before this time.*

(Keo, Arkansas July 6, 1890)

Mr. Morris won Kate. On July 31, he started to Virginia for the promised visit to meet Kate's family. Ten lines of his diary were left blank except for four words inscribed diagonally across the empty space. Uncharacteristically, he scrawled, "Having fun in Virginia!" He must have met the Lewis' approval. A month later, on September 11, 1890, my grandfather wrote in his diary very simply,

> *T11 Cloudy spent in LR started to Va to*
> *get married*
> *F12 Cloudy and Rainey, on way to*
> *Washington City*
> *S13 Cloudy arrived in Washington*
> *S14 Spent the day in Washington*
> *M15 left W for Fredericksburg, Va down*
> *River (Rappahannock)*
> *T16 arrived at Mansfield 11 a.m.*
> *W17 Clear bright married Miss Kate at*
> *9:30 a.m. and started to Washington*
> *T18 Washington*
> *F19 Clear & pleasant Spent the day in*
> *Washington sight seeing*
> *S20 " "*
> *S21 Went to church and left for St. Louis in eve*
> *M22 On B&O RR and in St. L 7p.m.*
> *T23 Cloudy in St. L sight seeing*
> *W24 " " " left for L.R. 9 p. m.*
> *T25 Rain last night arrived in L.R. 2:30 p.m.*
> *F26 Cloudy in L.R. home <u>with wife</u>*
> *S27 Cloudy & cool went riding in eve*
> *S28 Clear & cool at Home all day*

M29 Cloudy & dry Ride in eve

This is Mr. Morris' unembellished description of their wedding and honeymoon. I wonder if Kate had a church full of flowers with a "floral archway" and her "Rainbow of Hope" for the ceremony in St. Paul's at 9:30 a.m. I wish that I had an account of the service in Kate's own words, but I can only imagine what it was like. I do know that this early hour had become a traditional wedding time for brides in the Tappahannock area in order to board the daily boat that would take them to Fredericksburg for the train to Washington. Kate had her "Man of Men" and was off to Arkansas as Mrs. William Nathan Morris, wife of a prominent Arkansas landowner.

From the train in Little Rock, Mr. Morris took Kate to what he called their "country house" outside Keo, Arkansas. As he had promised, they rode horses together the next evening. In the month of September, the endless rows of stalks were bursting with cotton, illuminated in the moonlight like new fallen snow. Soon, mule-drawn wagons brimming with the white fiber would drive the two miles to the gin. Fall was a joyous time, a celebration of plenty. The air would have been clear and cool that night, and Kate must have felt that all of her dreams were coming true.

In the following weeks, Mr. Morris wrote in his journal and proudly underlined the words "Kate and I..." He took her to the small towns of England and Pine Bluff, Arkansas. There she enjoyed time with some of her old friends in the area where she had taught school. He went to Louisiana to acquire more "hands" to increase his labor

force. They had dinner at Dr. and Mrs. Donelson's home
and the Donelsons came to Keo to visit with them. That
first Christmas after they married, Mr. Morris wrote,

> *T25 Cloudy & cold at Home all day. Silver (the*
> *cook) sick. Kate and I got dinner. A very*
> *happy day at home.*

Mr. Morris continued his busy schedule. He wrote in
his ledger that on the farm they had planted alfalfa and
gathered corn and peas. They harvested the hay and hauled
cotton to his gin where it was processed and sold for nine
and half cents a pound. He bought eight mules and two
horses. He worked on mending fences and "deadening"
a field, a process by which a wooded area was flooded to
kill the existing trees and clear the land. He worked in his
Keo mercantile store and supervised his sawmill.

In the spring, "Old Boy" and the "gray mare" had a colt
and Mr. Morris again planted corn and cotton and cut clover.
He worried about floods, droughts, worms, and fires. He
made day trips by train to Little Rock (twenty-five miles
away), Lonoke (fifteen miles away), Pine Bluff (thirty miles
away), and England (five miles away). He attended con-
ventions, reunions, and expositions in Memphis, St. Louis,
Atlanta, and Texas. He rode his horse to oversee his land
and drove a buggy into town. He moved Kate in a wagon
from Sulphur Springs each summer and later from Keo to
Little Rock.

Eight months after the couple married, Mr. Morris noted
rather briskly in his diary that Kate had "discharged the
cook!" Mr. Morris had been married as a young man. His
first wife had died at a very young age. He had survived as

a bachelor for many years but had depended greatly on his hired cook, whose culinary ability was rich in the Southern traditions of her black ancestors. He probably enjoyed a close relationship with the woman who provided his meals for many years.

There were certain things that he obviously enjoyed from his past. He mentioned in his ledger that when the first frost came to Arkansas, it was time for hog killing. Pork was his staple meat. He wrote using exclamation points for emphasis about his delight in eating fresh peaches, garden peas, and snap beans, likely seasoned with plenty of pork fat. His usual daily diet had always been simple country fare.

Kate's family letters speak of wild turkey, "old ham" (what we know as the famous Virginian cured ham), cherry rolls with brandy sauce, fruitcake, and plum pudding—a little more elegant fare than Mr. Morris had been served at his table. Perhaps her tastes were turned to a more sophisticated menu or perhaps Kate was simply jealous of the cook's ability to please Mr. Morris.

THE FAMILY BEGINS

On April 12, 1891, Mr. Morris entered in his diary,
S12 Cloudy and warm, at Home all day
Kate little sick.

Around nine months later, on January 23, 1892, he recorded that Kate had a baby boy at 11:30 a.m. Mrs. Donelson
came to help and stayed five days. On March 13, he wrote,
that "Kate and the boy went out today," failing to mention
that their first son was named Frank Waring.

On Wednesday, May 11, 1892, when Frank was about
three months old, Mr. Morris whisked Kate away to Memphis for what he called "The Bridge Celebration," and
they stayed until Saturday. The historical Sesquicenten-
nial Supplement to the *Commercial Appeal*, May 25, 1969,
described the event.

> Steel girders across the Mississippi have helped
> make Memphis the area trade center it is. The
> first bridge, now known as the Fresno, solidi-
> fied the rail lines to the West. Its opening on
> May 12, 1892 drew a crowd of some 50,000.
> There were cheers as 18 locomotives chugged
> slowly across the span then returned at full
> speed, whistles blasting. The bridge, the only

one across the river south of St. Louis was the 3rd longest in the world and there was some doubt voiced about its load carrying ability. The railroad crews, all volunteers, incidentally proved the bridge's strength and time has underscored the verdict...It was primarily a railroad bridge, although wagon and carriages could cross on planks laid between the rails. This wasn't exactly encouraged. Most of the road traffic went by ferry.

Kate and Mr. Morris probably arrived in Memphis by ferry that day. Perhaps they stayed at the grand old Peabody or Gayoso Hotel. The event was the "place to be" in 1892. For Kate and Mr. Morris, the first locomotives thundering across that bridge were as dangerous and exciting as the first space launch.

On June 27, Mr. Morris recorded Frank's first tooth. On Monday, July 11, he wrote that at 11:00 a.m. Kate and Frank would begin their long journey back to Virginia to show Kate's first child to her family. She traveled by train to Fredericksburg and down to Tappahannock by boat.

My darling Husband;

My last letter was written on the boat. I got home safely a little after ten, Friday morning...Frank stood the trip better than could have been expected though still looks pale...he weighed 15 #. I have lost 2#...I lay down nearly every morning. I have gotten just a treasure of a nurse, she came this morning. I pay her $1.50 per month. She is a girl Sis Sue had for over the two years—is about 15 and is so reli-

able. She will wash and dress the baby, feed him &
do the cleaning up, so I can rest & grow fat, dear.
I do so enjoy the rest & I believe I will soon give
enough milk for Frank, already I see an increase.
My appetite is splendid. I drink a great deal of ice
milk. Then too Pa has dug a well in the yard & it is
such good pure water. I drink a great deal. My trip
was expensive. I did not spend even a nickel fool-
ishly, really did without when I ought not to have
done so. You see with a baby, I was helpless & had to
hire people to help me. I got home with just $9.00.
(Mansfield, Miller's Tavern, Virginia, July 18, 1892)

While there, Kate brought her first born to show him
off at St. Paul's Church.

Yesterday, we went to St.Paul's. How I thought of
the last time I was there when you were with me, as
we stood and were married…Well, I think your head
would have been turned forever if you had been there
and seen the fuss made over our boy. It was just as
you said it would be, "have you seen Kittie's baby?
Oh, he has the loveliest eyes you ever saw and is so
handsome." I did not get a pull at him except during
the sermon when he lay asleep in my lap. I wished
for you. We had the communion and oh, if you could
only have been with me. You know we have never
knelt together at the Lord's table.
(Miller's Tavern, Virginia, July 18, 1892)

Kate stayed in Virginia for two months, returning to
Arkansas on September 16. It was a hard trip. Frank and
Kate were sick most of the fall. Christmas Day 1892 was

very different from the family holiday festivities that Kate
had once enjoyed in Virginia. Mr. Morris wrote in his ledger,
S25 Cloudy and dreary at home all day.

In the new year of 1893, Frank was not well and Kate
was pregnant again. That winter, Mr. Morris recorded
more and more frequently, "Kate sick." There seems to
be more than the usual complaints of pregnancy. Physicians
were called in. The names of doctors appear more and
more in Mr. Morris' diary: Dr. Bash, Dr. Donelson, Dr.
Brittain "spent the night." Dr. Walters "here all night."
Dr. Robbins came.

Kate had complained back in 1885 of being extremely
tired when she came home from school. The fatigue continued though her letters along with frequent referrals to
her weight loss. Before she married, Kate had written to
Lumie in Mississippi,

> *Yesterday evening Mr. and Mrs. John Morrow were*
> *here and Mrs. Hinson and the whole crowd went out*
> *and got up on the scaffold where they weigh cotton*
> *and we were hooked up and weighed. I only weigh*
> *110, this time last year, I weighed 120 and every-*
> *body says I look badly.*

(Raineyville, March 2, 1885)

Mr. Morris had mentioned her weight loss in his letters before their marriage, on July 6, 1890.

> *You must weigh about 90 or 95 # by this time…I am*
> *afraid you will not be well enough to come to Ark as*
> *soon as we contemplated, the last of September, don't*
> *you think it would be better to wait until the weather*

gets cold. I think it would be a good idea for you to go to some good spa and spend the month of August and see if you can't regain your health again...

Like the word "pregnant," "tuberculosis," or "consumption," is never mentioned in Mr. Morris' diary or Kate's letters. Actually, not a lot was known about tuberculosis at the time. In 1865, Jean Antoine Villemin showed that the disease was contagious and could be transmitted by inoculation. The actual cause, the tubercle bacillus, was not discovered by Robert Koch in Germany until 1882. The only remedy that anyone offered was a cool, dry climate and rest.

The only possibility for such a treatment in the area was Sulphur Springs, Arkansas, seven miles from Pine Bluff and about forty miles from Keo. On Wednesday, April 26, 1893, Mr. Morris wrote in his diary that Kate went to Pine Bluff. He planted his cotton first then joined her there. On Saturday they went together to Sulphur Springs. This was his first mention of the summer resort.

Cotton Belt Railway sold tickets to Pine Bluff with bus transportations to Sulphur Springs included in the price. There was a fine hotel, a dance pavilion, and many planned social activities. In 1892, James Leslie, in his history on Pine Bluff, *Land of Cypress and Pine*, writes,

> ...Sulphur Springs bore a close resemblance to the high, pine-bearing land of Tennessee and the Carolinas from where many of the early Jefferson County settlers came...Some bought small tracts for summer homes...Some families moved to Sulphur Springs as soon as school

was out and did not return until that fall term began. Other families would stay part of the summer and then rent their cottages to other families...One reason the families spent the summers at the resort was so that the babies could breathe better away from the heat of the city. (p. 132)

One of Kate's brothers responded with some degree of caution,

Are you still taking baths? How long is the course of treatment? ...I might accept Mr. Morris' generous offer and try the sanitarium treatment for a while. It certainly must have done wonders for you. I am a great believer in massage. I believe it stimulates almost any part of the body to which it is applied and is such an aid to healthy circulation but it has to be done by trained hands and a wrong way of rubbing may prove injurious.

(Miller's Tavern, Virginia, 1902)

Mr. Morris undoubtedly moved Kate there for the summer. For the first time, long sections in his diary were left blank during July, August, and September.

On September 30, 1893, Frank fell and broke his arm. Kate was pregnant and not doing well. On October 19, the handwriting in Mr. Morris' journal is different. It is clearer and less hurried as though the writer has taken extra time to record the solemn event with thoughtful care.

T19 Our baby boy born, lived a few minutes.
We buried him at the Springs in the evening

M23 Clear <u>Came Home</u>

In November, Mr. Morris' diary was fairly normal. He moved their belongings from "the Springs" and Kate came home on the train, but she would have to face another tragedy all too soon.

S26 Cloudy rainy Frank sick Dr. Beakley sent for
M27 Cloudy at home
T28 Frank very sick
W29 Cloudy & cold, worse
T30 " " worse

On December 1, 1893
F1 Clear. Our darling left us this evening,
  safe in the arms of Jesus.
S2 Cloudy, We laid him away in the garden

When I was a child, my father took me out to the cotton field behind our house to show me the simple stone for his brother, Frank. It was comforting to find that it was hidden under the gentle shade of a large tree. I did not realize then that when he was buried there, it had been less than two months from the time that Kate had lost her second son in Sulphur Springs.

But, life went on. During the month of December, Mr. Morris went riding, killed hogs, gathered corn, and made three trips to Little Rock. Winter days amid the barren fields of Arkansas can be endless. The monotony of flat land is broken only by a few trees, black silhouettes against a gray sky. During this time of grief, Kate must have missed the gentle rolling hills of her home in Virginia more than ever before. She once wrote to Lumie, who had also lost her first child,

> *What a comfort to your heart to know when your little angel left your arms, he went to Jesus. There "safe in the arms of Jesus" he can never know pain or sorrow. His little soul free from the pollutions of earth is in heaven, waiting to welcome his father and mother. Our earthly ties one by one are severed: how much easier to bear our afflictions when we know those ties have only been transferred to heaven, only severed here to draw our hearts to God.*
>
> (Plum Bayou, June 6, 1886)

Kate and Mr. Morris spent their fourth Christmas in Arkansas alone at home on the farm near Keo.

By June 24, 1894 Kate was what Mr. Morris referred to as "sick" again. It was unusually hot, 102 degrees. Arkansas' summer heat sent waves rippling across the scorching cotton plants, causing the view of the landscape to move like liquid in the July sun. The air was still and stifling. On July 28, Kate and her husband returned to Sulphur Springs, and Kate stayed there for most of the summer. Mr. Morris traveled back and forth to his farm by way of Pine Bluff. On October 4, when Mr. Morris wrote in his diary that it was "clear and cool" again, Kate returned to Keo. On Kate's fifth Christmas in Arkansas, the doctor was called in to see her. The entourage of physicians continued to come.

On January 21, 1894, Nannie Lewis arrived in Keo. Kate's beloved forty-six-year-old "old maid" sister, fifteen years her elder, had always been like a mother to Kate.

PICTURES

WILLIAM NATHAN MORRIS

KATE AS A YOUNG TEACHER
IN ARKANSAS

KATES' SONS – WILLIAM AND EDWARD

KATE AND HER DAUGHTER, ANNIE

WILLIAM, ANNIE, LEWIS, EDWARD

AFTER KATE'S DEATH
LEWIS, ANNIE, MR. MORRIS, WILLIAM, EDWARD

AFTER KATE'S DEATH
MORRIS CHILDREN ALL ATTENDED KEO SCHOOL
EDWARD-3; WILLIAM-4; ANNIE-24; LEWIS-28

MAIN STREET, KEO, ARKANSAS 1909

St. Paul's Church, Essex County, Virginia

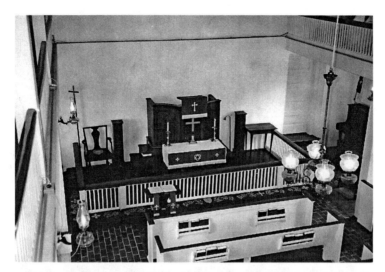

INSIDE ST. PAUL'S

INSIDE ST. PAUL'S EPISCOPAL CHURCH
BENCHES IN BALCONY WHERE SLAVES ONCE SAT

WARNER LEWIS, KATE'S PATERNAL GRANDFATHER

KATE'S MOTHER AND FATHER AT ST. PAUL'S
ANN URSULA LATANÉ AND THOMAS WARING LEWIS

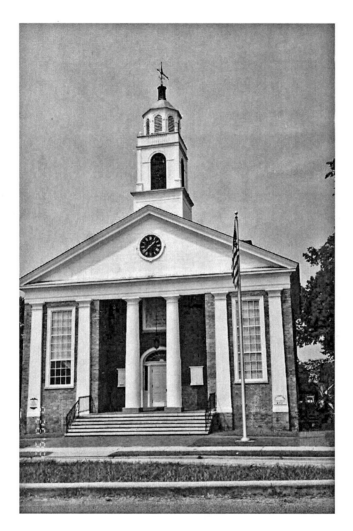

ESSEX COUNTY COURTHOUSE,
TAPPAHANNOCH, VIRGINIA

INSIDE ESSEX COUNTY COURTHOUSE

HENRY WARING LATANÉ 1782-1860
KATE'S MATERNAL GRANDFATHER

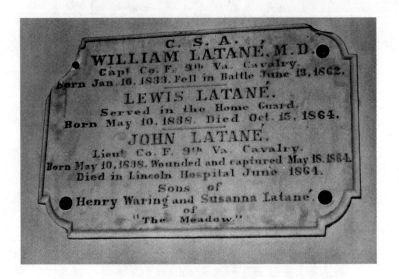

KATE LOST THREE UNCLES IN THE CIVIL WAR
PLAQUE INSIDE COURTHOUSE

THE BURIAL OF LATANÉ
BY WILLIAM D. WASHINGTON
INSIDE COURTHOUSE

Ann Suzanna, or "Nannie," was plagued by arthritis for years, but she lived until 1922, outlasting most of those who nursed her through the years. In 1901, Kate's other spinster sister, Lucy, wrote to Kate. Her description of Nannie, all wrapped in flannel, brings to mind a Hogarth rendering.

> *I am so thankful to tell you Sis Nannie continues to improve, her general health is right good but she is still very stiff. I walk her about the room about four times during the day. I have to support her as she walks. A few days ago I was very much delighted when she took two or three steps alone...Susan seems amused at the way I fix her up at night. She wears outing gowns. I make her a colored saque of outing which she wears over the own gown. I take off her flannel drawers & put on heavy pants (that Julie Jones gave her) & then she sleeps in stockings. I have fixed caps for her knees of red flannel which she wears day and night. So you see she ought to be comfortable.*

(Miller's Tavern, February 7, 1901)

In 1894, seven years before this letter, Nannie was still up to the demands of a trip to Arkansas from Virginia. She probably suffered some very painful arthritis even then, but the determined lady came to see that this "confinement" would go well and Kate would at last have proper care.

Nannie set to work immediately. On February 1, Mr. Morris wrote that he went to Little Rock, house hunting. By the time their third son, Edward, was born on February 26, Kate was ensconced in her comfortable, warm home on Arch Street in Little Rock. Dear, dear Nannie remained with Kate until April 4 when she was sure that Edward was healthy and safe.

Kate's father revered his daughters and was careful to see that they were protected. Originally, he stated that any of his daughters who did not marry would inherit the home and land for their use as long as they lived. After Kate married, he revised his will to read, "Upon mature reflection of Thomas Waring Lewis I do give and bequeath my farm on which I reside known as Mansfield to my daughters, Ann Susanna Lewis ("Nannie") and Lucy Catesby Lewis during their lives, they having the privilege of using or for sale every kind of wood on the said farm, this I do as a token of my love and affection for them in their tender care and devotion to me in my declining years..."

Nannie was not the only one to visit Kate. Her brothers Thomas and John and her sister Susan Smoot made the trip to Arkansas to see Kate. Her sister Mary would later come to live in Keo when her husband joined Mr. Morris as a partner in a mercantile venture. Kate managed the long trek back to Virginia with her children four times in the seventeen years of her marriage.

That summer, Kate and Edward went back to Sulphur Springs and stayed until the last of September. Mr. Morris continued to travel back and forth, sometimes remaining several days at what he called "the springs." On August 15, there was an eightieth birthday celebration for Kate's father at Mansfield in Virginia. In a printed speech given on that occasion, Kate's brother-in-law, Phil Lewis, stated that eleven of Mr. Lewis' twelve children were present. That fact must have been difficult for Kate who was the only missing child.

On October 6, Mr. Morris left for an exposition in Atlanta and stayed for six days. He returned on October 12 as Kate was leaving for a two-month stay with her family in Virginia. She came back on December 12 to spend her sixth Christmas in Arkansas. Mr. Morris' diary entry on December 25, 1895, recorded the fact that they had Christmas dinner with his brother, James, in England, Arkansas.

January and February of 1896, Mr. Morris bought ten mules, went "horse hunting," or shopping the market, killed hogs, and ploughed the fields in preparation for spring planting. March in Arkansas can be bitter cold. Springtime is evasive. The hours weigh heavily while the land remains frozen, waiting to be planted. In 1896 it snowed on March 12.

On March 19, Kate's younger brother John Latané Lewis arrived in Keo. He was a thirty-one-year-old physician who later practiced medicine in Bethesda, Maryland. Perhaps he came as a family representative to review Kate's physical condition. He returned to Virginia after eight days.

The day after he left, a Dr. Baskenville came to call. On May 28, Mr. Morris moved Kate back to Sulphur Springs. It was another summer of trips back and forth between the farm and "the springs." Mr. Morris recorded on June 1896 that Kate was "a little sick again" expecting another child.

At the end of this ledger, Mr. Morris composed, or copied, a rather badly written poem with no title. Poor as it may have been artistically, it must have expressed his despair and his determined commitment to duty.

> When things don't go to suit you
> And the world seems upside down
> Don't waste your time in fretting
> But drive away the frown

Perform your duties without a frown
Will make your pathways bright and clear
Falter. Stop and leave undone
Will make it like the clouded sun

In September, Mr. Morris took a buggy to Sulphur Springs and moved Kate back up to Little Rock to her home on Arch Street for the winter. He returned to Little Rock in a buggy on December 24 and spent Christmas there with Kate and Edward. He stayed a week because he caught a cold. The trips back and forth to Little Rock and the farm seemed to keep him at a frantic race most of the time. The new year brought new hope and a new life into the world. My father, William Nathan Morris Jr., was born on January 26, 1897. Mr. Morris wrote in large capital letters:

T26 Cloudy & very cold. Temp 19 deg.
BABY BORN, WILLIAM

Kate, William Nathan Jr., and Edward remained in Little Rock probably with a nurse. Mr. Morris continued to make the trip to the farm. He always considered his home to be in Keo and seemed delighted when, on May 28, he recorded that he "came home" with "Billy and Kate." In June he wrote that he went down to the town of England and proudly underlined "With Kate!" He returned to Little Rock with her and remained the last half of July.

August on a farm is "lay back" time. There was nothing to do but wait for the cotton to be picked. It was a good opportunity for Mr. Morris to take Kate to spend two weeks in Hot Springs, Arkansas. They did not return to Sulphur

Springs that summer. Maybe Kate was feeling better. That fall, Mr. Morris seems to have stayed more often with Kate in Little Rock where they spent Christmas Day.

The next year, 1898, brought the death of Kate's gentle father, Thomas Waring Lewis. On February 9, Kate wrote a letter to her sister Mary in Virginia. The tone of her writing is very different from that of the young, carefree girl who wrote to Lumie. The symptoms of a chronic illness were growing more apparent:

> *I did not put on the very deep mourning, Mr. Morris seems so anxious about my health. I know he would oppose it. I don't know what is the matter but I am so thin & I look 5 years older than I did last Sept. I have a cough that gives Mr. Morris great anxiety but I think it is needless. I had the Grippe in Oct. & every since, I have had a cold and cough most of the time, just as I think I am getting over it, I take fresh cold. I have not been sick though at all; can stand more than I ever did in my life. If you could see this great big baby, I think you would say my flesh has all gone to him.*
>
> (1400 Arch Street, Little Rock, Arkansas, February 9, 1898)

Symptoms of tuberculosis continued to appear in her letters, "prolonged cough for more than three weeks," "loss of appetite," "weight loss," "pallor and often a tendency to fatigue very easily."

That spring, Kate summoned all of her strength to start for Virginia with her two sons on May 3, perhaps to have William christened. She returned to Little Rock on June

30. In July, Mr. Morris made a business trip to Memphis and Mississippi. It is fascinating to learn of the mobility that their family enjoyed in the late nineteenth century. I am amazed at the incredible stamina of Mr. and Mrs. Morris in covering all of those miles.

On October 1, Mr. Morris mentioned that a Mr. Lewis arrived from Virginia and accompanied him to Keo to see the farm. In November, he wrote in his diary,

> *T22 Cloudy & cold went to farm,*
> *Mr. Lewis took charge*

This meant that Mr. Morris had engaged the husband of Kate's sister, Mary Latané Lewis, to assist in his farming operations. Previously the couple had left their home in Virginia and headed west when Phil became Minister of Indian Affairs for the United States government in the Dakota Territory. Their baby had the distinction of being the first white child born in the territory. Their granddaughter in Arkansas had many Indian artifacts and governmental papers concerning this portion of their lives. Mary had insisted that they come back to Virginia to have the twins that they were expecting at the time. Finding a position in Virginia may have been very difficult, so it is natural that they would come to Arkansas where they had family and a potential job. Mr. Morris' journal and letters often mention the Lewis presence in Arkansas. Mary was a great source of strength and comfort for Kate.

Mary and Phil would later return to Virginia, but their daughter, Annie Lewis, eventually married a Mr. Carl Lee Cobb of Keo and lived there on his farm the rest of her life. I remember Cousin Annie with her curly red hair, her bright laughing eyes, and her vivacious charm. In this faraway Arkansas land, she never lost her strong Virginia accent with her "owuts" and "abowuts." Her brother, Dr. John Waring Lewis, served in the Philippine Islands as a naval physician and brought us a beautiful silk embroidered portrait of a lion. He lived in Keo for a while and later made rare, coveted visits. My mother and father reminisced about how much fun it was to be with this cousin they called "Jack."

At the end of December, there is another line in the diary, "Kate is sick." In June 1899, Mr. Morris traveled by train to Dallas and Sherman in Texas. There was a barbecue supper in Keo on July Fourth. In Mr. Morris' journal, the whole month of August is blank except for one boldly underlined entry squeezing in his brother's visit and the birth of another son. There was no weather report:

W16 Bro Ed & wife came, born to us a boy

Lewis Dean Morris was their third living son and Kate's fifth delivery. She was thirty-five years old. For most of the month she moved with her three boys back to Keo and, on Christmas, they spent a "pleasant day at home."

The year 1900 was a year of sick children. Mr. Morris repeatedly wrote in his journal, "Edward sick...William sick...Lewis sick... All sick!" Mr. Morris was by now fifty years old. It is no wonder that he left his family in Little Rock while he stayed in Keo to handle his business.

The year 1901 quickly fulfilled Kate's secret dream. She had a little girl on January 3: Annie Latané Morris. Kate's married sister Sue Smoot wrote to her, saying,

Many congratulations to you, the mother of a baby

daughter...the long looked for came at last.
(Miller's Tavern, January 15, 1901)

In February, Mr. Morris went to St. Louis to a meeting. In June, Kate's sister Sue came from Virginia for a visit. In July, Kate returned to Virginia and stayed for a month, returning to Arkansas on the fifteenth of August. In September, Mr. Morris' diary faithfully recorded that President McKinley had been shot. In December, Mr. Morris spent ten days with Kate and his family in Little Rock for Christmas.

In April, Mr. Morris left for Dallas to attend a family reunion. His busy, demanding life continued, but the frequency of Kate's illnesses was increasing. Reality had to be faced. She was diagnosed with tuberculosis. Stronger measures had to be taken to find the best treatment available at the time.

SEARCH FOR THE CURE

I n her book *Blazing the Tuberculosis Trail*, Jean Abrams wrote the following:

> The history of early Colorado conjures up images of untold wealth, boom and bust, fortunes made and lost in silver and gold and the great rush that led to the founding of a territory... As early as 1860, hundreds (and later thousands) flocked to Denver and Colorado Springs to "chase the cure" to seek remedy for tuberculosis, the most dreaded disease of the era. Indeed, tuberculosis held the dubious distinction of being the leading cause of death in nineteenth century America...No single accepted standard for tuberculosis treatment prevailed in the early years, but by 1880 medical opinion emphasized fresh air for respiratory tuberculosis ailments. Colorado, with its dry and sunny climate, drew tuberculosis victims like a magnet...while demand for proper accommodations increased... as more and more arrived to chase the cure, services did not...Consumptives who had flocked to Denver in hope of finding cure were unable

to secure simple lodgings, let alone medical
care…a patient bitterly wrote, "Colorado is most
glad to welcome the contents of the purse the
invalid brings with him, but she would greatly
prefer that the invalid should not accompany
the purse." (p. 2)

Because of the mild, dry climate, New Mexico had also
become a popular health resort. Several friends from the
farming community in Keo such as Mr. Aticus Cobb, who
is mentioned in one of Kate's letters, had already gone
to New Mexico to find a cure and later resumed a normal
life. It was most likely his recommendations that directed
Mr. Morris and Kate to Dr. Howse's boarding house in New
Mexico. From March 19–29, 1903, Mr. Morris wrote:

T19 Cloudy Started to New Mexico
F20 Cloudy On way to N.M.
S21 " Arrived in El Paso, Tex
S22 Clear & Cool at EP went to NM
M23 " " Las Breezes NM
T24 " " "
W25 Cloudy & Rain " "
T26 Clear & Cool " "
F27 " " Started home from N Mexico
S28 " " Left ELP for Home
S29 " " on way home arrived in LR 9 ½ o'ck

There are no recorded details, but it must have been
a harrowing five-day trip with four children. Edward was
nine, William six, Lewis four, and Annie was two years
old. I have heard family stories mentioning the fact that

they took a nurse or maid with them. Kate refers to Nora in one of her letters. I try to picture this fifty-three-year-old father, very ill mother, four young children, and the endless miles to Mexico. On the ninth day, Mr. Morris left Kate and the nurse alone with the children in one of the many boarding house "sanitariums" in Las Cruces, New Mexico.

The first letter that I have from Kate in New Mexico is written on stationary with letterhead that reads, *THE ALAMEDA, open all year, John R. Howes, M.D. Prop.* The conditions must have been less than ideal and the credentials of the physicians quite questionable.

> *My darling husband,...Annie seemed in a stupor and did not want to dress...I called in Dr. Howes in that night...he assured me that she was doing alright and that I need not be uneasy...The next morning Dr. Howes came in early and said she was alright. She had fever all night and still lay in that stupor, so after he was gone, I was so uneasy I just could not stand it...we called in Dr. Gerber from Las Cruces. He is a very young man but I certainly do like him. He examined Annie very thoroughly...after a very careful study of the case, he pronounced it an aggravated case of indigestion, told me to give her two more grams of coloment, and he left two kinds of medicine and do you know, she wanted to dress before night...It made Dr. Howes very angry for me to call in this other DR. He has not spoken to me since dinner yesterday, hasn't inquired about Annie. It is very silly in him. I am sorry he takes it so but I have no apology to make to him. Three boarders left this week and Forest Cobb (from Keo) said he was*

going Monday. I am not going to stay here. The Dr. has said nothing about letting me keep house and he has been drinking a good deal lately. I know it would not be pleasant...
(...I have seen the Dr. again and he is alright.)
(Almeda, Las Cruces, new Mexico, May 16, 1903)

My Dear Husband, had a talk with Dr. Howes this morning and I hope at last everything is settled. He agreed to let me keep these two bedrooms and take a little room over the other house for a kitchen that opens into a sunny nice little reception hall but off from the rest of the house which I will use as a dining room, he furnished me with a table, chairs, dishes, silverware, a cook stove, everything complete, a little ice box and a horse and cart, the one Mr. Lamb had, all for $30 per month. I also have the use of his phone. I think that is a very fair bargain, don't you? He will fix up everything so I can begin housekeeping next week. I think we can be very comfortable here. He has gotten the boys another bunko. He did not buy it, just keeps it for the feed. We were compelled to make a change—and I can live cheaper here and I really believe gain more than anywhere else, unless I could put up in a first class Hotel somewhere else, could not do that with the children—I like the Vinol so much. I can see already that the accumulation of phlegm is not so great—I am hungry all the time when we go to keeping house I am sure I will do just fine—Now you just hurry up and come, and I will be so happy. I do hope I will get the check

> *tomorrow—I will owe Dr. Howes $75.00 and of*
> *course want to pay up before I stop boarding.*
> (Almeda, Las Cruces, New Mexico, May 22, 1903)

The "bunko" is probably a built-in frame that has low sides to serve as a bed and makeshift sleeping place for the boys or a storage bin for their clothes. Dr. Howes had used it for a grain bin in the past. Her letter continues:

> *I am just beginning to show the effects of this cli-*
> *mate—I did not write you much about myself be-*
> *cause I was afraid you would get discouraged about*
> *me…I felt all of the time that I would get well here.*
> *I at one time weighed 94, I weighed today and weigh*
> *98 ½ since taking the Vinol my cough is so much*
> *improved. I want to keep that up all the summer.*
> *We ate dinner today in our own little dining room*
> *for the first time. It was a pleasure. I went and got a*
> *supply of groceries. I find some things are very high,*
> *butter 35 cents and eggs 30 cents.*

I discovered an historical Vinol advertisement on the Internet for "puny children." Vinol would "build them up, make them strong and robust." The single ingredient listed was "Wine of Cod-Liver–Oil." The claims continued, "Try on our Guarantee/When the Blood is Poor/When More Flesh is needed/When the Weak Need Strength or/ The Throat and Lungs Repairing." Vinol was a cod liver oil preparation for coughs, colds, throat and lung troubles, but the label indicated that it contained 14 percent alcohol, which would certainly not have been safe for children. A May 6, 2010, article in BrandlandUSA Blog, "Remembering

Vinol the Drug for Anemia," stated that Vinol's popularity in the late 1900s was due to clever business advertising by large drug companies such as Chester Kent and Drugs Inc. They had convinced Kate.

Obviously the "miracle drug" she praised in her desperate search to find hope would offer her no permanent relief, but Dr. Howse had given her the accommodations that she had requested. All seemed wonderful for Kate, or she pretended that it was in her letter to husband.

I am sure that Mr. Morris quickly recognized the ruthless practices of this charlatan physician. After three months, without any explanation, Mr. Morris wrote in his diary on July 5, "Kate came home." That winter, all of the children had the measles and Mr. Morris spent Christmas in Little Rock.

Kate's sister Mary Lewis came to help Kate in Little Rock on the first day of January 1904. Kate was sick almost all of March. On June 7, Mr. Morris wrote at the top of his diary, "Kate starts for Denver." He did not go with her this time but sent her alone with the nurse named Jennie. He was preoccupied with problems on the farm. The spaces in his diary are not concerned with his wife but record the steady rise of the Arkansas River. When the water reached twenty-nine feet, he wrote, "The country all under water." He lost his stand of cotton and had to replant, but somehow he prepared to go back to Denver on July 8. Kate had been away a month. He left at noon on the ninth and arrived in Denver at 2:30 p.m. on the fourteenth. He stayed with Kate until August 8.

There were multiple problems with Kate's accommodations in Colorado. The house she was renting was advertised for sale. Not only were strangers coming through the house, but she was anxious about having to move at any time. She was afraid to buy fuel for more than a month.

...Rouse is a rascal will do anything for money. He knew these radiator pipes leaked before he went away. I haven't gotten the man up here yet and it is raining now and cold. I am afraid to tamper with the thing. If there isn't enough water in the pipes the whole thing is likely to blow up and it certainly does leak so I will try to make the fire till the man comes. I wish you could see this Hagan House and see what you think about it. Mrs. Mcdonnell said she thought it was reasonable. Mr. Hagan told me Sunday, he would sell the house furnished except the piano and some pictures, suppose you write to him making him a cash offer, that is if you think it practical to buy. The cellar is finished.

(577 High Street, Denver, Colorado, October 8, 1904)

Kate and Mr. Morris were realistically facing the fact that this was no temporary arrangement. It would take time for healing. The prospects of getting better were growing dim. Mr. Morris owned a house in Little Rock, one in Keo, and was renting another in Colorado. They made the decision to rent out the Little Rock house with the arrangement that one room would be reserved for Mr. Morris' use when he was in town.

I can see from your letter today you are somewhat bothered about the house. Well I want you to do what will make you comfortable. We don't know a thing about those people and you will have to be particu-

lar about what you leave out and take a list of all household goods, especially bedclothes, pillow, etc.... So have Annie go up and pack away things. (I have sent a list) and make the best most comfortable trade you can.

(577 High Street, Denver, Colorado, October 8, 1904)

I am so glad to hear you like the people and hope they will make you comfortable when you go up. I wish you would look in the little wash stand in the little room and you will find my little writing desk, please put it away—I have letters I prize so highly in there, several from my father.

(577 High Street, Denver, Colorado, October 18, 1904)

Annie was Kate's cousin from Virginia. She was married and lived on a farm outside of Keo. She would be the most trustworthy person to make decisions for Kate. There is something final and sad about this request. This writing desk probably contained many of the letters that Kate so carefully saved for me.

Mr. Morris and Kate had settled the problems with the house in Little Rock but in Colorado her worries turned to the schooling of her children. Kate had always been concerned about the Christian education of her children. That is why she wanted to have a house in Little Rock. In this weary letter to her husband, she is considering sending the children to a private Episcopal school in Denver. She is physically unable to tutor them anymore.

I did not get a letter from you in reference to money. You spoke of the children going to school. Having

*them here all day to contend with, some nights, I feel
exhausted from the conflict, they are so noisy and
this house is so small. It would be much better for
me if I could take a walk every morning at the time
I teach them.*
(577 High Street, Denver, Colorado,
December 14, 1904)

Kate wrote her brother Reverend Thomas Dean Lewis
in Virginia to ask his advice about an Episcopal school
in Denver for her children. Thomas had graduated from
William and Mary College and the Episcopal Theological
Seminary at Alexander where he received his Doctorate
of Divinity. In the middle of his long advice-laden letter
to his sister, he drifted into a most enthusiastic account
of his recent trip to Washington where he met the Archbishop of Canterbury. At the time, Thomas was thirty-five
years old, four years younger than Kate. He was preaching
regularly at St. Paul's Church in Tappahannock.

Kate must have longed to be near her family where
these exciting incidents were happening beyond her dreary
and hopeless attempt to regain her health. Colorado was
even farther away than Arkansas. It must have been with
some degree of sadness that she read her brother's exciting
account of the Archbishop of Canterbury's arrival in Washington to attend the open-air ceremony on the grounds at
Mount St. Alban's where the National Cathedral would
one day stand. Thomas wrote,

*While I was in Washington, I had the great privilege
of attending the open air service at which the Archbishop of Canterbury spoke. Thirty-five thousand people*

were present and a procession of clergy bishops and ministers and choir all vested to the number of 900 or 1000. The service was held in an open space in a large grove of oaks on a high hill overlooking Washington & the Soldier's House on the Potomac. The music was soul-stirring. As the vast procession came singing Jerusalem, the golden one could not keep back celestial visions. The archbishop's address was hearty & earnest & made a fine impression. Bishop Doane's service was very inspiring. He made a beautiful appeal for the home. I also had a card of invitation to a reception given the archbishop by the church's Men's Club of Washington so that I met him..."

In answer to the questions about the education of her children, which was always foremost in her mind, he wrote,

My dear Kittie; I was glad to get your letter several days ago and was delighted to hear you had entered the boys in Wolf Hall. I heard of the school repeatedly while I was in the West and know that work done there stands high. I do not think the cost is at all high for that kind of school. It is so important I think that children should have the best of teachers when they are small as well as when they become advanced in their studies. And nothing on earth takes the place of a positive Christian education such as boys get in the church school. One of the reasons I believe so many young people grow up irreligious is because religion is divorced from their education whereas no education is helpful which does not point to the Author and Source of all of our Knowledge and depends in us a sense of responsibility for the higher use of our light and Knowledge. My experience in observing men is that it is very very rare that they ever outlive the influence positive and honored through life of a school which has its daily worship and its teaching of Bible & church History. It is instilled into the mind and grows into the character.

I am glad Mr. Morris does not oppose this attendance at the Episcopal School. I feel with you that you cannot afford to let them lose the influence from church… if the time ever comes that he did not want them at a church school then you would have to supplement their school education with Bible and church teaching.

(Miller's Tavern, Virginia, November 4, 1904)

Thomas cautioned his sister to obey her husband's wishes concerning this matter. Kate was determined about her boys attending a good Christian school. She must have had her way, for William, age seven, wrote a letter to his father mentioning his attendance at Wolf Hall. He had not quite mastered the art of spelling or punctuation yet.

Dear Papa, I will write to you today. I haven't been feeling very well today. I am going to be a good boy now Mother is feeling well today I did not go to school today I have the sore throat our teach is going to mak a big stocking and hang it up on the wll at Wolf hall we are going to give present to each other we went downtown to see Santy Claws last Saturday We have bin having a good time at school

(577 High Street, Denver, Colorado,
December 13, 1904)

On September 26, Mr. Morris attended the World's Fair in St. Louis and stayed a week. Life went on for him. In Colorado, Jennie (the nanny Kate had brought with her) was homesick, worried about her mother, and having a problem getting into night school. Kate begged Mr. Morris to come.

> *I feel so happy at the prospect of having you a month, the time will pass quicker having that to look forward to.*

(577 High Street, Denver, Colorado, October 18, 1904)

> *I suppose you will start next Wednesday, a week from today. I am very sorry you feel you are making such a sacrifice to come, it will make us all feel rather uncomfortable to know you feel you are losing money by your visit. I think you make a mistake in having so much work to do—You have done the work of about three men ever since I have known you...It is not my judgment to keep on paying such big rents, unless money was no object and it is. I have to economize in every way possible. I haven't bought me a thing, not five cents worth of clothing for myself since I left home except my coat and I paid for that with the money James sent to me. I do hope I can do my own cooking in six months and do away with the girl's hire. I haven't gotten anything for the children yet for Christmas, will get one toy around, the last of the week. Have you any cheap handkerchiefs in the store? If so please bring me a doz for the children. I hope we will be well when you come and can meet you at the depot.*

(577 High Street, Denver, Colorado,
December 14, 1904)

Mr. Morris did not come. He wrote in his diary that Arkansas' Governor Eagle died on December 20 and that he had Christmas dinner in England, Arkansas, with his brother George. It was February 4, 1905, before Mr. Morris started for Denver. He stayed two weeks and three days. In May, he wrote that the boys had come home with him but Annie stayed in Denver with her mother. He waited until the crops were "laid by" and then took the boys back to their mother in Denver. All of this traveling had to be difficult for him. He returned home alone to Keo on September 16, 1905.

The next pages of Mr. Morris' diary are fragmented, with only the bottom portion remaining until November and then all are missing. As I read his faithful daily accounts, I sometimes found that a few aging pages were worn away or nibbled by some unknown creature, but this last portion of the 1905 diary seemed as though it might have been ripped out of the ledger. I found no diaries for the years from 1906 to 1911 but in that year, his faithful record keeping resumed in the existing records from 1911-1919. His last one-line entry on June 25, 1919 was, "Down with arm Pain." He died on July 17.

With no diary entries for 1906 or 1907, I had no record of Mr. Morris' activities during the last year of Kate's life except a minor mention of his name in one of her letters. In order to complete the final chapter of Kate's life, I found three letters saved in a single envelope. It was as though some guided hand had set them apart for the purpose of closing Kate's story in her own words.

The first letter was dated March 27, 1906—seven months after Mr. Morris' last diary entry—from St. Anthony's

Hospital in Denver. It was written by Kate to her sister Nannie in Virginia. I had once read the writing of a young, carefree girl and later a joyous new mother. Now I had the privilege of reading Kate's words at the end of her life. She was only forty-three when she was in a Denver Catholic hospital critically ill and alone. It was a beautiful letter. There were passages like poetry when she described the "silent black-robed sisters, gliding in and out who seemed a part of the unreality of it all." She expressed the power of prayer that brought a sudden peace and contentment: "and from that hour, the improvement began." This temporary recovery gave her a little more time on earth with her children, which she accepted with gratitude.

> *My Darling Sister;*
> *I address this to you but it is for you and Annie both. I have been trying to write to you but am beginning fresh today, hoping I can finish it. You don't know how near the "border Land" I have been since I wrote. I am perfectly sure all that saved my life was being brought here just when I was. I knew there was a <u>chance</u> of my getting better and as long as there was, I would not write how sick I was. But to lie here alone hour after hour, only when it was necessary for some one to attend to my wants then to see the silent black-robed sisters glide in and out seemed a part of the unreality of it all. I would get so excited I could only by great effort control myself. Yet if Dr. Hopkins came in took my hand just the contact would soothe me then when he left, I would cry like a baby, but no one knew it. He had the sister to rub me with alcohol that would sooth me too, just the touch of*

human sympathy quieted me. But no one could stay with me all the time. The nights were simply hideous when I longed so for the touch of some one who loved me. For three days I had no hope at all. I would even get out of that bed and Oh! Sis, Mary, may you never know the horror of feeling you are going to die among strangers. I thought of so many things I wanted to tell you, so many directions about the children. I see a death bed is not the time for them so as soon as I get home, I shall write you a letter and leave it to be sent you in case we never meet again. I have had several direct answers to prayers this year and I want to tell you of the one while I was so sick. It seemed so hard for me to leave my children and I prayed all one morning to be spared for them that never again would I murmur because I had to be banished this way from all I love and suddenly in the evening, I just felt like there were so many other prayers being offered for me and such feeling of contentment came over me and from that hour the improvement began—and so I have learned at least to be content to live wherever I have to stay and at last can say, "Lead thou me on." I have met with a great deal of kindness here. The Sisters have really petted me and Dr. Hopkins has been so good, and my friends have come to see me oftener than I expected. This is about six miles from where I live. I have had flowers and fruit brought me. How I am up and can walk around some and am not so lonely as when I was in bed. But I have to be so very care-ful. Sunday the girl brought the children over and I

walked around a little with them in the building and
yesterday had fever again but I lay down most of the
day and have had more today.

Wednesday Morning
I got so tired I had to stop yesterday, so will finish
this morning. I had a talk with Dr. Hopkins late
in the evening, he says, I am doing well now but
every precaution must be taken to prevent another
breakdown like this, his expression was the chances
are you would go under the next time...that I cannot
stand so many breakdowns. He does not want me
to leave here till I have arranged something for the
three boys. I am trying to see if I can get board for
them for awhile any way. He says there is no use my
saying one word. I absolutely can <u>not</u> get any better
and have the care of four children. When I came here
Dr. Sewell said if I had proper care, there was no
reason why in two years, I should not be able to
live anywhere. Dr. Hopkins said the same. You see
I have been here nearly two years and am very little
better than when I came. I have improved at times
wonderfully, then would have a breakdown, have
had three serious ones. Last summer, I felt so strong
and well then you see after I had all the children, I
broke down again. The boys are just as sweet and
good as can be and E & Wm considerate far beyond
their years—and it nearly breaks my heart to give
them up. Yet it is my <u>only</u> hope of life. Dr. Hopkins
promised me he would write to Mr. Morris today. I
hope he will. Bro. Eb has recently written offering to

*take the boys. Poor little Lewis, he is just a baby and
I have won him over so this winter. So often now he
comes and hugs me and tells me he loves me. I can't
tell yet what my own plans will be. My dearest love
for you, each one. My next will be to Annie. Your
devoted sister, K.L. Morris*
(St. Anthony's Hospital, West 16th Avenue, Corner
Quitman Street, Denver, Colorado)

Less than a month later there was a second letter from
Kate to her sister Mary who was living in Keo, Arkansas,
near Mr. Morris. Now she was well enough to be out of
the hospital and living back in her rented rooms at 570
Gilpin Street. The boys were being cared for elsewhere in
Denver by a Mrs. Nobles since Dr. Hopkins told her that
she could not risk living with the children until she was
stronger, but she was able to visit them and keep up with
their activities.

*My dearest Sis, Mary,
I wish you knew how much I enjoyed your dear letter. I wanted to answer it at once but have had so
much company to come in and have to rest when
I am tired. I am gaining faster now. One marked
change I see since the boys left is in my sleeping. My
normal nights rest since first of Jan. has been five
hours, often three or four and so nap during the day.
Once in a while I slept all night from exhaustion.
Now, I sleep often 8 hours and can take a nap during
the day. My nerves seem more quiet. I do miss the boys
so. They have spent both Saturdays and Sundays with
me. I had them to come last Saturday to prepare*

the ground for me to plant some seed and they did it very nicely. They want to continue at this Sunday School so I told them they can come early and attend it and spend the day here. I feel that it is best to do that, they are under my influence and don't disregard the Sabbath. Please write me what Mr. Morris says about it. He wrote me last week to put the boys on the train and send them to him. But I can't help thinking the present arrangement is best for the present at any rate. I talked with Mrs. Noble over the phone. She says the boys are so good and haven't given her any trouble. She said they were never out of her sight. She keeps them night at home after school hours. I have not been strong enough to go to see them yet. Yesterday, (Easter Sunday) we had some exercises for the children at the tent. Annie recited the 23 Psalm and Edward had an Easter piece. Each child was given a blooming pansy in a little pot. E&W took theirs to their boarding-house, said they have a big south window and they want them in it. I have just gotten Mr. Morris' letter and will write to him some time today. I also got a letter from Sis Sue, saying Mr. Smoot is a good deal worse. I am so sorry to hear it. Sis, Mary, have you ever thought of his having cancer of the stomach? Please don't hint this to her but she wrote of his having nausea all the time what with his great weakness and inaction does point to cancer. I hope not but I feel very uneasy about him now. Life seems so full of trouble now for so many years our lives flowed along so evenly. We all had our trials of course, but no great sorrows and now since Sis Lucy's death, we seem to have lived in the shadow of some sorrow all the time. I am so grateful to you for your sweet letter. You know I never hear any words of affections there are never any caresses and sometimes my heart just seems starving and the weight of it all nearly crushes me and you in your full life can hardly realize how empty mine is and how happy a little of love, sympathy and appreciation of my efforts makes me feel as yours did last week.

How is Annie? I hope she is getting on better now. And you haven't mentioned Waring for so long. Where is he? Did he decide to leave Keo? I would give so much to see you and Annie. I think so constantly about Annie. Write whenever you can. With a heart full of love for you each one, Your devoted sister, K.L. Morris

She added a postscript,

I saved you one of Lewis' chickens, he just takes the scissors and a piece of paper and cuts them out without out a pause or any previous drawing. His teacher drew one on the board & showed them how to cut them. I think he shows talent.

(April 16, 1906)

Kate was determined to be with her children as long as possible and continue to take part in their learning process. As ill as she must have been, she remained vitally interested in all of their activities and tried to participate, but it is clear from their own letters to their father in Arkansas, the children were pretty much on their own.

My grandfather had carefully guarded these letters from his children who express in their innocent words more than I could ever write.

Dear Papa, I have been intending to write to you for a long time. I love you. How are you getting on? Your loving daughter, Annie Morris (age 5)

***

Dear Papa, I love you. How are you? I would like to see you, Lewis (age 7)

***

Dear Papa,
We have had a snow, but it is not very deep. Mother is better. The cook has left and we are doing our own cooking: The washerwomen cam today and washed all of the things nicely she is coming back tomorrow to iron. The furnace is a very good one. It keeps very nicely all we hafto do is to open up the drafts and then we go upstairs and dress, then we come down stairs and put some more coal in the furnace. Then we make a fire in the cook stove and then cousin Blance cooks breakfast. We have to wash the dishes before we go to school. We have early breakfast so we can wash dishes,
Your son W.M.M. (age 9)
(Denver, Colorado, November 2, 1906)

***

Dear Papa,
I have been intending to write to you but have not done so. It snowed today but melted as fast as it fell. Mrs. Hopkins is going to rent their house and move over to one Colfax. They are going to give us their

"blue" rabbits. Mother is much better! We are all well including Cousin Blanche! Mother is eating ice cream and broth and biscuits! Florence Lincoln is lending us books to read at night. The nurce has just told us that she is eating custard and tea!
Will close
Your loving son
E.E. Morris(age 12)
(644 Gilpin Street, Denver, Colorado, November 2, 1906)

These letters show how much the children had to bear with their mother in the hospital, but they did it with great maturity and courage. It would not be long before they were on their way home with their very ill mother. I have to wonder how she could make the trip back to Arkansas on a train with the children in her condition, There were no more letters nor any diary entries to give a time line and account of what happened between November 2, 1906, and Tuesday, December 17, 1907, when Kate's obituary appeared in the *Arkansas Gazette* in Little Rock, Arkansas.

> Mrs. Katherine Morris, wife of W.N. Morris died 9:40 o'clock yesterday morning at her home, 1400 Arch Street. Death was caused by consumption from which she had been an invalid for almost five years. Mrs. Morris was born in Virginia. She had been married about 27 years *(actually 17 years)* and leaves her husband, three sons and one daughter.
>
> The funeral will be held at 2 o'clock this afternoon from the family residence, in charge

of Rev. G. Gordon Smede. The body will be
buried in Oakland Cemetery.

Kate's faithful sister Mary, who had moved to Keo
with her husband when he came to work as a manager
for Mr. Morris, was at her side until the end. She wrote
to her sister Nannie in Virginia describing Kate's last day.
This letter to Virginia had somehow made its way back
to my father and was saved for me.

Darling Nannie,

I suppose of course you all have Phil's telegram &
letter telling you of dear Kitty's death which took
place Mon. morning at 1 o'clock the 16th. And it is
sweet to think of her as being at rest after so much
suffering so often she would say, "how I long for
rest, sweet rest." She was entirely conscious up to the
last breath & died a most triumphant death, said
death had no fears for her, all was well but asked me
to hold her hand until I thought she had reached the
other shore. She took leave of each of the children and
talked to them. She kissed William's hand (she would
not let any one kiss her face for fear she might give
the disease) & told him she appreciated his waiting
on her & said, "the Lord will bless you for it." [My
mother once told me that William, my father, would
follow the ice truck to catch the shavings in his hands
before they fell to the street, then race inside with his
frozen treasure before it melted to bathe his mother's
fevered face.] She then thanked the nurse and called
for Livie up close to the bed and made her promise
to stay there & take care of the children & keep them

together, then thanked Livie for her kindness to her, then said, "Livie, this is a voice from the grave you hear." She was not a bit excited & had the sweetest smile & her eyes were oh! so bright & she would look in the most loving and longing way at me, hold my hand & said, "You hold my hand here and Sister Lucy is on the other side to take it when you let go." It seemed that all the wells of love & affection that had been pent up for so many years were opened the last few days & she just longed for love. She would take my hand & smooth it. So often she said to me, "My good and kind sister, you have stood by me" and said, "don't be afraid to die when your time comes. I will be at the other shore to welcome you home." The last week of her life it was very cold weather, rainy, damp & Oh! so chilly—The Dr. told me my health and the nurses depended on plenty of fresh air in the room so we kept two windows open & the room door open. I never suffered so much with cold in my life & we both took bad colds but thought that was better than getting the germs. You see, Kitty never had a Dr. until about two weeks before her death and there had been no precautions taken against germs. The neighbors would come in every day to see her but they told me they were afraid to be in the room long at a time. Cousin Mollie would come and stay a short time but she was afraid to sit up. The nurse & I took it by times and did the sitting up & nursing. Cousin Mollie was with me at the end, she had told me to phone for her & she got to the house about 5 minutes before the end. She was such a help & comfort—Kitty had

asked me to get a cream cashmere shroud for her & I had been down & selected it, so Cousin Morris & Mr. and Mrs. Ebb Morris went down & selected it, the coffin & shroud. Mr. Ebb Morris helped Dr. Smeade in the service which was conducted at the house & it was full and oh, Such lovely flowers! The grave was entirely covered. I kept out a few to send to you. She was interred in Oakland Cemetery in Little Rock. Mr. Morris bought a section. Lena Fox and Mrs. Donelson came up from Pine Bluff to attend the funeral. A good many went up from England. I asked Dr. Smeade to send a notice to Kitty's death to the Churchman, your ever devoted sister, M. L. Lewis.
[Mary Latané Lewis]

(Keo, Arkansas, December 18, 1907)

In another envelope, I found a small black and white photograph of the children standing with their father on the front porch of a house in Keo. Judging from the ages of the children, it must have been soon after Kate's death. The yard is barren and stark. The faces are all somber and sad. The life and light of Kate were gone. There was one unsigned letter inside the envelope, written in the familiar penciled handwriting of Mr. Morris to a lady, only identified as "Miss B." It must have been his desperate attempt to find a mother for his family.

Dear Miss, I have been thinking for some time of writing to you and let you know how we are getting on. The children are going to school and are doing fine to have no one to look after them. It seems impossible to get you to come and live with us. I have been thinking of asking your permission to come to see you and see if I could not prevail on you to come and live with us if not as Miss B. maybe as Mrs. M. Of Course, I know but little of you but I think I could love you, for it is my nature to love anyone who is good and kind which I know you would be. I need some one to share my Joys and my sorrows. Am almost dying to have someone to love and care for. The children need the care of a mother at this time. More than they will ever need one so I hope you will think kindly of this offer and consent for me to visit you soon.

Perhaps this was only a rough draft of his thoughts and a formal copy was never mailed. If Mr. Morris did mail such a letter to Miss B, she must have refused his offer or come as a hired nanny, for he never remarried.

When his daughter, Annie, was old enough, she was sent away to Galloway, a girl's boarding school in Searcy, Arkansas. The boys continued to attend the rambling old wood-frame schoolhouse in Keo until they graduated from high school. A photograph of Keo High School's small student body includes all three of the Morris boys and their sister, Annie. Upon graduation, each one was sent away to Hendrix College, a Methodist school in Conway, Arkansas, which was an institution that Mr. Morris had strongly supported all of his life. In a Hendrix College publication, framed in my cousin's office, the school president paid a great tribute to him after his death for his lifetime generosity to his church and those in need and included this comment, "His last days were days of suffering. He was seen to walk hour after hour on his veranda, holding his right arm which later fell limp at his side, the bone completely eaten away." This could have been a form of bone tuberculosis. He died in 1919, twelve years after Kate. He left his land to be divided among his four children.

As I wrote the final pages of "Finding Kate", I discovered a letter tucked inside one of our family Bibles from my father, William Morris to his sister, Annie, while serving in the Navy during WWI on the battleship USS Texas. She had sent him the previously quoted letter (p.102-104) from his Aunt Mary Lewis after Kate's death, written some fifteen years earlier. His response expresses the lasting impression that my grandmother had made on him, even after her death. The respect, admiration and love shine through every word. It confirms the powerful influence that this tiny lady from Virginia had on all of her children through her resolve and devotion to her family.

Dear Sister:

I received your letter this morning, and I appreciate so much your thoughtfulness in sending that letter written by Aunt Mary. It has indeed been an inspiration to me. It makes me realize and wake up to the condition I am letting myself slip into and going so far below the heights I should have attained with such a wonderful mother we had.

In this life, a man rarely takes time to think about his own soul, you know what I mean, just go off by himself and think back and realize how the world is carrying you, to sit down and think what might have been and what a different person you could be. In other words, take a deep look down in your soul and see yourself as you really are. This seldom happens unless it is something like this letter that awakens those thoughts. I can see again that death chamber as plainly as if it were yesterday and can remember now tho I had forgottn how mother looked when she called us in and to say goodbye for the last time. Oh! how my heart aches and my conscience smites me when I think what a heavenly angel our mother was and what she expected of us. It hurts me more I suppose than any of the rest of you. I don't suppose Lewis and Edward give such things a thought and you have fulfilled mother's ideas in every respect, and I want to say here that I am very proud of you too. But with me she expected more than the other boys, mainly because I waited on her more , but what I did was the least I could do and I don't think I deserve any credit for it. Anyway, she seemed to have great hopes in me and now when I think what I have turned out to be, it makes my heart fairly bleed with remorse. Just think what different children we would have been had she lived to keep us as she started. As much as I have been mixed with the world, I have never encountered anyone who had anything to compare with our early training. It has not all been in vain either, I am glad to say. Sometimes I forget it but its influence still remains tho a good many times, I don't take heed to my convictions. There is always something within me no matter how hard I try to crush it down, that warns me and tells me when I am doing wrong and I contribute this to what our mother taught us in early life.

When I think of how Papa must have suffered at the loss of our darling mother and what a shadow it cast in his life , and after all how bravely he faced it all, how he tried so hard to bring us up as he knew Mother would have done, and how trying it must have been on him sometimes. I then know what a wonderful father we have been blessed with. I know God's blessing will be bestowed on him.

As I write here to nite, it seems as tho I can feel the spirit of our darling mother very near me. A feeling that has seemed dead in me for years, but your letter started me thinking and I feel tonight a happier and closer touch to those things that are sacred and holy, than ever before in life. I feel that, her guardian angel will look after us and that someday we are all going to be united on that other shore. It makes me rather sad and melancholy to think about such things but then on the other hand I have such a happy and glorious feeling that I smile thru the tears and say—all is for the best and I'm going to try to do my best from now on. Again, sister, I want to tell you I am glad you sent that letter and it is a prize that I shall always keep. I wonder if Aunt Mary remembers writing that? She described things so real and beautiful, it's almost like a vision from the other world.

Must say good nite sister and may God bless you,
Your brother,
William

***

On April 26, 2009, I returned to my childhood church to attend the Keo United Methodist Church Centennial Celebration. The small white clapboard sanctuary had been built on land that my grandfather had given in Kate's memory soon after she died. William Nathan Morris Sr. played a major role in establishing the church, and many of his children and grandchildren have continued to be the leaders and major supporters of the church, which has miraculously survived these hundred years. Though none of their own children were alive on that long awaited Sunday, six of Kate and William Nathan's nine grandchildren attended.

Edward Everett Morris' oldest daughter, Mary Morris Cardwell (Mrs. Verla Ray Cardwell) was there. Edward's only son, Edward Nathan Morris, was present with his wife. Mary Cardwell's daughter, Gloria Stachurcki, gave a history of the church. Edward's other two living children, Dorothy Morris Capps (Mrs. Rex Capps) and Florence Juanita Morris, were unable to make the celebration.

William Nathan's son, Robert Waring Morris came with his wife from Little Rock. I drove there with my husband from our home in Memphis, Tennessee. (A sad note for us was that our oldest brother, William Nathan Morris III, had passed away at age sixty-five in 1989. He lived in Keo most of his life and never failed to attend Sunday service and the Sunday morning men's breakfast meeting, a custom that continues to this day.)

Lewis Dean Morris' only son, Lewis Dean Morris Jr., whose home is located immediately behind the church, arrived promptly as he usually does on Sunday morning.

Annie Latané Beard's only daughter, Bonnie Sue Beard Evans, flew in from Houston, Texas, for the ceremony.

It was quite an auspicious occasion, as the Methodist Bishop of Arkansas, Reverend Charles N. Crutchfield, delivered the sermon to us. Even though it was not an Episcopal ceremony, I think Kate would have been very proud. In a sense, it was a tribute to her and the love that Mr. Morris held for her. Although the years seem to have covered over every trace of our grandmother, Kate's spirit and deep faith in God lives in all of her grandchildren. Many of them have remained in the community and continue to farm the same land that belonged to their grandfather.

I think of all the letters and of all the members of family and even strangers who saved them over the years. Perhaps it was that last little "tug" or warning that made someone stop and put a note or letter back in a drawer and say to themselves, "Not yet!" Somehow, I always felt that these words were saved for me, so I could tell Kate's story. There is something wonderful and magical about that.

Kate's youngest brother, Thomas Lewis Sr., wrote to my father when he was in the U.S. Navy during World War I:

> *I have always followed you children with interest for your mother had me to baptize you & take its vows of godfather for you...I copied a letter in the type-writer for you which your mother wrote me not very long before her death, before she left Denver. It is a beautiful letter and I know you would be interested in it and touched by the allusions to you all—you and Annie. She was a saintly and beautiful character. I know her prayers are a blessing and a protection*

110

around about you today.
(Sweet Briar College, Sweetbriar, Virginia,
May 21, 1917)

I never found Kate's letter that Thomas Sr. typed for my father, but as I read the one above, I guess I assumed that her prayers were not only a "blessing and protection around" my father but for me as well. I felt that my grandmother was always here with me as I wrote her story.

Kate's own gold-leaf framed engraving of the *Burial of Latané*, which survived a serious fire in my mother's home, now hangs in my entrance hall. A happy circumstance brought the original painting in brilliant color to the Dixon Art Gallery in Memphis from July through October, 2009 as a part of a touring exhibition featuring American Art of the Civil War Era. I went to see it often, for it was like having a private visit with Kate, Thomas, and the family.

Much later in my search, I drove to Little Rock to visit Kate's final resting place at Oakland Cemetery in Little Rock. I had never been there and only found it through the obituaries that I had acquired from outdated Little Rock newspapers. It was an old cemetery. The cold stone mausoleum stood alone and seemed abandoned, seldom frequented by a modern world. The aging stone vaults in the silent structure that held Kate and Mr. Morris side by side were not where I wanted to leave them. I knew that I must finish Kate's story and bring her back into the world she loved among the family she left far too soon.

As my quest to find Kate drew to a close, I realized that, from the beginning, it had been Kate who had found me. She led me on quite a chase, through libraries, cemeteries, churches, courthouses, and attics where she not only left me with a deep appreciation of my heritage and my family but showed me the power of her unwavering faith in God.

She was a pioneer, a teacher and a missionary during her often sad journey through life. Most of all, she was a mother whose deep spiritual strength gave her the power, even in death, to remain a part of her children's life as long as they lived. Her extraordinary influence has blessed every generation . Through her courage and persistence, she earned her own place of honor in the family's illustrious history.

I once met a young relative of Kate's modern descendants. He had attended and sent his children to Virginia schools and remained there throughout his adult life. He admitted that he saw no reason to stray beyond the borders of his home state. Virginia had everything he would ever need and he was content. Kate ventured forth with a passionate pride to find more than living on her family's reputation and to discover her own world. She, however, remained anchored by her deep Virginia roots with her firm convictions and faith in God wherever she might be.

Within the pages of this book, I hope that I have captured the spirit of Kate and passed on to future generations the inspiration and positive joy in her life. Thank you , Kate, for reaching over the miles and the years to become such a good grandmother to me and to all of us.

THE FAMILY REUNION

Rarely in the history of a family do the records show such a day as that spent at "Mansfield", the residence of Kate's father, Mr. Thomas Waring Lewis, of Essex County, Virginia, on August 15, 1895. It was the anniversary of his 80th birthday.

Thirty-three of his nearest kin, among them eleven out of a family of twelve children, were gathered together to extend their hearty congratulations and gratifying assurances of the everabiding character of the truth and integrity which his life has daily imparted through precept and example.

The large company assembled under the shade of the beautiful grove of poplars to partake of a bountiful repast. Before leaving the table, Dr. Warner Lewis in a few well-chosen remarks spoke of the occasion which had called us together and announced that Mr. Phillip W. Lewis would make the congratulatory address. He was followed by Dr. Thomas Latane, Rev. Joseph Lewis, and Dr. William L. Lewis.

About 3 o'clock the company assembled for a service of prayer and thanksgiving which was conducted by Revs. Joseph and Thomas D. Lewis, the closing prayer being offered by Dr. Thomas Latane.

The services closed with the hymn, "Blest be the tie that binds our hearts in Jesus' love," and as we parted we felt that it was the power of that love that had protected us and held us united through years of separation.

We give below the address of Mr. P.W. Lewis, in full,

Honored Sir:
Ladies and Gentlemen:

Few can appreciate more fully than we do today the pleasures incident to this occasion, and seldom do we see so many relations of one man as we have before us.

In the language of the gifted Daniel, at the unveiling of the Minor bust at the University of Virginia not long since, so I will say today, "Unlike Mark Antony we come to praise Caesar, and not to bury him".

We have come from different portions of the Old Dominion, from Maryland, and from the far off land of the setting sun to extend to you our congratulations on this the EIGHTIETH ANNIVERSARY of your birthday and with our congratulations, our best wishes for a continuance of these blessings which a kind Providence has bestowed upon you. Few men attain the ripe old age which you have reached and fewer still—pardon me for the allusion—have reached that age with a name untarnished and a character above reproach as you have done.

These should be held dear by every man for "He who steals my purse, steals trash, but he who steals my good name takes that which he cannot return".

Honor, chivalry and integrity have been held sacred and respected in every age, and no man has done more than you, Sir, to instill these qualities in his off-spring and posterity.

As we gather today to congratulate you, we all bear testimony to that honor which has always characterized you in your dealings with you fellowman and to that integrity and uprightness of life which have so often been taught to us and held up to us by you as the landmarks which should characterize the Christian gentleman and the patriotic citizen.

Aye, and in you case it has extended further, outside and beyond the circle of your friends and acquaintances and has developed into an honorable and patriotic allegiance to your country, and a faithful performance of your duty to you God.

Your chivalrous nature and unbounded admiration for the ladies have always characterized you, and no man under Heaven would be more willing to uphold the women of our land than you, and none ever held her in higher reverence, and in greater respect and esteem.

This gathering of relations reminds me of ante-bellum days, when children and grandchildren loved to meet at dear old LEWIS LEVEL to celebrate the festivities of the Christmas holidays. In those good old times the cares of life were laid aside, and the dear old grandfather, long since laid to rest, threw open wide the doors of his grand old mansion and gave up all to those who came to enjoy his unbounded hospitality.

You, Sir, were among the grown up people at that time, while I and a host of others were among the children of those happy days.

Fond recollection has often carried me back and time and time again have I lingered around the ancestral home, where sacred thoughts cluster, and boyhood scenes "bring back fond memories of the past". "Times change and we change with them". The glories of "Goldberry" and "Lewis Level" have departed and the "old home is not what it used to be. Its inmates have scattered and left alone, it has gone to decay.

You, Sir, and one of two others here and there, are the dear old landmarks of a past generation whom we delight to honor and associate with, while we who were youths at that time have grown up to manhood and womanhood and assumed the responsibilities of life.

Your immediate family has given to the world representatives of the Ministry, the Bar and the Medical Profession, and you no doubt look upon their work with pleasure and with pride and remain at home the "Noblest Roman of them all".

(150 copies reproduced by Tom Lewis for the 1985 Lewis reunion)

LATANÉ LINE OF ASCENT

1. JEAN CAROLYN MORRIS
   (7 APRIL, 1932-   )
   – William Eugene Long
   (4 October, 1927-   )

2. Generation – WILLIAM NATHAN MORRIS
   (26 Jan 1897-23 Nov, 1981)
   – Mary Martha Murchison
   (31 Jul, 1902-28 Jan, 1985)

3. Generation – William Nathan Morris
   (01 Jun, 1845-15 Jul, 1919)
   – CATHERINE LEWIS
   (26 Feb, 1863- 16 Dec, 1907)

4. Generation – Thomas Waring Lewis
   (15 Aug, 1885-21 Jan, 1898)
   – ANN URSULA Latané
   (05 Nov, 1826-06 Nov, 1876)

5. Generation – HENRY WARING Latané
   (29 Jul, 1782- circa Jun 1860)
   – Ann Susanna Allen
   (circa 1797-circa Oct, 1878)

6. Generation – WILLIAM Latané
               (circa 1750-circa 1811)
               – Ann Waring

7. Generation – JOHN Latané
               (11 Oct, 1722-circa 1773)
               – Mary Allen

8. Generation – LEWIS Latané*
               (circa 1672 [in France]-circa 1732)
               – Mary Deane(circa 1685[in England]-11 Jun, 1765)

"Parson" Latané

LEWIS LINE OF ASCENT

1. JEAN CAROLYN MORRIS
   (07 Apr, 1932-   )
   – William Eugene Long
   (04 Oct, 1927-   )

2. Generation – WILLIAM NATHAN MORRIS
   (26 Jan, 1897-23 Nov, 1981)
   – Mary Martha Murchison
   (31 Jul, 1902-28 Jan, 1985)

3. Generation – William Nathan Morris
   (01 Jun, 1845-15 Jul, 1919)
   – CATHERINE LEWIS
   (26 Feb, 1863-15 Jul, 16 Dec, 1907)

4. Generation – THOMAS WARING LEWIS
   (15 Aug, 1855-21 Jan, 1898)
   – Ann Ursula Latané
   (05 Nov, 1826-06 Nov, 1876)

5. Generation – WARNER LEWIS
   (13 Dec, 1786-14 Jul, 1873)
   – Ann Susannah Latané
   (07 Nov 1791- 07 Jul, 1822)

6. Generation – JOHN TALIAFERRO LEWIS
   (?   -14 Jul, 1872)
   – Susannah Waring

7. Generation – CHARLES LEWIS
   (25 Feb, 1729/30-circa 1770)
   – Lucy Taliaferro-

8. Generation – JOHN LEWIS
   (circa 1694-17 Jan, 1754)
   – Francis Fielding
   (circa 1700-27 Oct, 1731)

9. Generation – JOHN LEWIS
   (circa 1669-circa 1725)
   – Elizabeth Warner
   (circa 1672-circa 1719)

BIBLIOGRAPHY

Abrams, Jeanne. *Blazing the Tuberculosis Trail.*
Denver Colorado Historical Society, 1991

Brown, William M. *Episcopal Mission in Arkansas.* New
York: Church Mission House, 1915

Cocke, Christine McRae, "Matilda Wright Haile," *Essex County
Historical Society News Letter,* 14:5, November, 1978

Goodspeed Publishing Company. *Biographical and Historical
Memoirs of Pulaski, Jefferson, Lonoke, Faulkner, Grant,
Saline, Perry, Garland and Hot Springs Counties, Arkansas.*
N.p.1889

Jones, Leslie, *Cypress and Pines,* Rose Publishing Company
Inc., 301 Louisiana, Little Rock, 1974.

Slaughter, James B. *Settlers, Southerners, Americans: The History of
Essex County, Virginia 1608-1984.* Salem, West Virginia.
Walsworth Press, Inc.1986.

Sorely, Merrow Egerton. *Lewis of Warner Hall.* Baltimore:
Genealogical Publishing Co., Inc., 1991

Thomas, David Y., Ed. *Arkansas And Its People, A History,
1541-1930.* New York: The American Historical Society, Inc.,
New York, 1930

Women's Club of Essex County, Ed. *Old Homes of Essex County.*
Richmond: The Williams Publishing Co., 1957